N. C. Edwards

The Jewess of Heidleberg

N. C. Edwards

The Jewess of Heidleberg

ISBN/EAN: 9783337138035

Printed in Europe, USA, Canada, Australia, Japan

Cover: Foto ©ninafisch / pixelio.de

More available books at **www.hansebooks.com**

THE ACTING EDITION.

THE JEWESS OF HEIDLEBERG,

OR,

THE FALL OF THE INQUISITION.

A THRILLING DRAMA IN FIVE ACTS.

DRAMATISED BY N. C. EDWARDS.

WITH CAST OF CHARACTERS, STAGE BUSINESS, COSTUMES, RELATIVE POSITIONS, &c., &c.

BUFFALO:

GEO. W. REESE, BOOK & JOB PRINTER, 148 MAIN STREET,

1866.

Entered according to Act of Congress in the year 1866, by
N. C. EDWARDS,
In the Clerk's Office of the District Court of the United States for the Northern District of New York.

Positively this Drama is not transferable.

CAST OF CHARACTERS.

Sir Martin Wilsdorf.—A Knight of Germany.
Bardolf Eberswald.—His Esquire.
Berthold.—The Margrave of Baden.
Conrad of Marburg.—The Chief of the Inquisition.
Sir Joseph Verdin.—Grand Master of the Brotherhood.
Victor of Antioch.—Deputy Grand Master.
Hector.—Lieutenant.
Baldwin of Tyre.—A Knight of Tyre.
Michael Forstern.—an Inn Keeper.
Andrew Fornbach.—an Inn Keeper.
Walter.—A Spy of the Inquisition.
Therwald.—A Spy of the Inquisition.
Jacob Olsheim.—Father of Eleanor.
Moses, } Jews of Heidelberg.
Anselma, }

Soldiers, Familars, and Brothers of the Steel Cross.

Eleanor Olsheim.—the Jewess of Heidelberg.
Irene.—Niece of Victor of Antioch.
Theresa—Wife of Michael Forstern.
Margaret.—Wife of Andrew Fornbach.
Chambermaid.
Katrina.—A Domestic.
Calypso.

STAGE DIRECTIONS.

R. means Right; L. Left; F. the Flat or Scene running across the back of the stage; D. F. Door in Flat; R. D. Right Door; L. D. Left Door; F. E. First Entrance; C. Centre; S. E. Second Entrance; U. C. Upper Centre.

₊ The Reader is supposed to be on the stage facing the audience.

ACT I.
Trial by midnight of Bardolf of Eberswald.

ACT II.
Death of Jacob Olsheim.

ACT III.
Escape of the Jewess of Heidelberg.

ACT IV.
Death of the Spy of the Inquisition.

ACT V.
Destruction and fall of the Inquisition.

COSTUMES.

WILSDORF.—Doublet, with belt and sword in sheath around the waist, knee breeches, tights, shoes with buckle, cape attached to doublet, hat with white plume, gauntlets

EBERSWALD.—Short Doublet with white collar, knee breeches, russet boots, hat with black feather, sword, &c.

BERTHOLD.—Ankle boots, tights, knee breeches, doublet with hanging sleeves, hat with feather, red domino, mask, &c.

CONRAD.—Suit of black, black domino, with tinsel cross.

VERDIN.—Suit of black, sword.

VICTOR.—Brown suit and sword.

HECTOR.—First dress, black domino with red cross—Second dress in fifth act, last scene, black suit and sword.

BALDWIN.—Same as Victor.

MICHAEL.—Brown doublet, knee breeches, grey stockings, shoes.

ANDREW.—Ibid.

WALTER.—Black Doublet, with cape attached—broad brimmed hat, with black feather—knee breeches, and russet boots, sword, &c.

THERWALD.—Black Domino and Red Cross, Sword, &c.

JACOB OLSHEIM.—Figured Robe—long grey hair and beard.

MOSES.—Brown Gown.

ANSELMO—First dress, black gown—Second dress, tattered dress.

FAMILIARS OF THE INQUISITION.—Black dominos, red cross and swords.

SOLDIERS.—Doublets and knee breeches, boot tops, shoulder sword belts, with sword, helmet, &c.

ELEANOR.—Sky blue silk dress, the hair to be worn in curls.

IRENE.—Boys dress to suit the times.

KATRINA.—Servants attire

THERESA—Brown dress and cap.

MARGARET.—Black dress, cap, &c.

CHAMBERMAID.—Common attire.

CALYPSO.—Dark brown dress and cap.

SCENE,—GERMANY.
THIRTEENTH CENTURY.

THE JEWESS OF HEIDELBERG.

ACT I.

SCENE 1.—*Martin Wilsdorf's Apartments—Armor hanging on wall—table and chairs,* L.—*A fireplace,* R.—*Window,* R. F.—*a Door,* C. F.
BARDOLF EBERSWALD *discovered sitting on a chair,* R.—*Thunder and lightning*
[*Knock,* D. F.
BARDOLF *opens the door.*]
   Enter SIR MARTIN WILSDORF, *muffled in a cloak.*

Mar. Zounds! This is a storm in very deed. [*takes off cloak and lays it on a chair.*]

Bard. By our lady, you may well say so, my master. The rain has beat against our windows until I verily thought the glass would be driven in; and the thunder has sounded as though the peaks of the Schwarzwald were tumbling to pieces. But you are wet and cold. Shall I put a fire in your chamber?

Mar. No, Bardolf. Bring me dry clothing, and I will get rid of the wet and chill while you are preparing supper. [*exit Bardolf,* L. 2. E.—*takes a chair and sits by the fire.*] The Margrave is getting too bold. Though he is my pupil he treats me like his slave; but I think he will find that Sir Martin Wilsdorf will not much longer be his tutor.

  Re-enter BARDOLF, L. 2. E. *with dry clothing.*

Bard. Here is your clothing, and you can be putting them on while I see about your supper.

Mar. That is right, Bardolf. I must confess that I do feel quite hungry. Try and be as quick as you can, [*exit* BARDOLF R. 2 E.—*puts on dry clothing.—Re-enter* BARDOLF, R. *with supper on a tray.*] Ah! good Bardolf you are quick.

Bard. [*Puts a white spread on table and then the supper.*] That is what I am always.—It is all ready, so come and take a seat.

Mar. [*sitting by the table and eats.*] Has there been any person here this evening?

Bard. No, good master; nobody was here. Why, do you expect any person to night.

Mar. No. But as I was going a little ways above here, I met a man coming from this direction. So I thought he might have been here and enquiring for me. I did not speak to the man because he did'nt seem to notice me. [*Thunder and Lightning.*] This is a great storm—but, good Bardolf, have you had your supper?

Bard. O! yes.

Mar. That is right. And I must tell you, whenever you feel hungry, you can eat as much as you choose. [*rising.*] Well, I'm done; you can clear the table. [*Bardolf clears the table and exeunt* R.] [*Goes to window and looks out. Re-enter* BARDOLF, R.]

Bard. Egad, Sir Martin, this is a doleful night. [*Lightning.*]

Mar. A doleful night—a doleful day—a doleful year! [*goes to* c.] What sort of a country do you call this?

Bard. A fair country, sir, is it not?

Mar. So fair, Bardolf, that I have a mind to leave it.

Bard. What! leave Baden?

Mar. Aye, and leave Germany too.

Bard. You are out of sorts, my master; what has gone wrong?

Mar. What has gone right?

Bard. Why, much has gone right. You are famous. Even the Margrave himself comes to you for instruction.

Mar. Not so, Bardolf. The Margrave sends for me to come to him.

Bard. But you are his tutor?

Mar. Yes.

Bard. And how does he succeed?

Mar. Bah! How can I do that which nature has failed to accomplish.

Bard. What has nature to do with making a swordsman?

Mar. Nature has much to do with making a man!

Bard. Certainly.

Mar. But she has not made a man of Berthold. He is a wretch!

Bard. And methinks, he has plenty of company.

Mar. Aye, that he has; and I would be rid of them. In truth, good Bardolf, I believe I shall ere long bid adieu to Germany.

Bard. And whither will you go?

Mar. To some land where there is a Christian ruler.

Bard. Is there not a Christian ruler here, my master?

Mar. Who rules in Germany?

Bard. Frederic is Emporer.

Mar. Then why is he not with his people? Why is he hidden away in his Italian Kingdom, following pursuits that are only fit for girls and tender headed boys! By Saint Paul! Frederick is not ruler in Germany.

Bard. Who is ruler then?

Mar. Conrad of Marberg! [*Bardolf crosses himself.*] The Inquisition has become the governing power in Germany, and the chief inquisitor absolutely holds the reins of government. Do I not speak the truth? Lives there a man in the empire, outside of the holy office, whose life is not in the hands of Conrad and his red handed familiars?

Bard. [*Looking around the room.*] Zounds, my master! if Conrad of Marburg could know of your bold speech, your head wouldn't be worth a straw.

Mar. Exactly, Bardolf; and the fact that you speak the truth proves the truth of what I have said. Should you inform against me, I——

Bard. Hold, Sir Martin. By the mass, I'll not listen to such speech. *If I inform against you!* Why don't you ask me if I would cut off my own head! [*a knock,* D. F.] Holy Lady! who can that be on such a night as this?

Mar. Go and see.

Bard. Suppose it should be the black-robed inquisitors!

Mar. Pshaw! The inquisitors don't trouble themselves to go about the streets after their victims. Make haste and don't keep the applicant too long in the storm. [*Bardolf opens the door. Thunder and Lightning,*]

    Enter VICTOR OF ANTIOCH *and* BALDWIN OF TYRE.

Vic. We seek Martin Wilsdorf.

Mar. I am the man.

Vic. We would speak with him alone.

Mar. Bardolf, you will please retire. [*Bardolf exuent,* R.] Gentlemen, I am Martin Wilsdorf, and this is my home. If you seek shelter from the storm, you are welcome. If you come on business, I am ready to listen.

Vic. We are alone, I think.

Mar. Yes sir.

Vic. Let us be seated then, and speak understandingly. We are strangers to you, though you are not a stranger to us. For the present you may know me as Victor of Antioch. My companion you may call Baldwin of Tyre. Do you wonder at our names?

Mar. Not at all, [*drawing three chairs to* C. *and all seat themselves.* The meaning of your visit affords me wonder enough for the present. And still, the names of Antioch and Tyre recur to me with many wonderful associations.

Vic. [*Throwing open his coat and shows on his vest a cross.*] Perhaps you know the meaning of this?

Mar. Ha! you know Henry?

Vic. Yes.
Mar. He was your friend?
Vic. He was my brother.
Mar. How fares it with him now?
Vic. He has my prayers and my gratitude.
Mar. What more?
Vic. My implicit obedience to his laws.
Mar. Where did you meet him?
Vic. In the Holy land.
Mar. How?
Vic. On my knees.
Mar. Did you take his hand?
Vic. I did.
Mar. How?
Vic. [*Falling on his knees and takes Martin's hand.*] Thus
[*They converse together.*]
Mar. We meet, three knights of the cross and sword, and by the laws of our order we are friends and brothers even to the death.

Vic. Ah, Wilsdorf, I might put you to a severe test.
Mar. Try me.
Vic. I might place my life in your hands.
Mar. Then my own should be staked for its safety.
Vic. [*Taking a steel cross from pocket which has a point like a dagger.*] Do you know the meaning of this?
Mar. Is it a cross or a dagger?

Vic. Both! It may be a cross for the just, and a dagger for the unjust. Would you know more?

Mar. Yes.

Vic. First answer me one question: Are you friendly to the inquisition?

Mar. By the Holy cross! If you were Conrad of Marburg himself, I would answer you—No!

Vic. Martin Wilsdorf, if I reveal to you a secret which might place my life in your hands, will you swear by your honor as a Knight of the Cross and Sword, that no word or sign on your part, shall betray me, or betray any part of the secret?

Mar. I swear, solemnly.

Vic. I thus trust you in this directness of approach, because there was already a sacred bond between us. Know ye that there is a secret organization in Germany destined to wield immense power against wrong and oppression of every kind. For the present its aim is the crushing of the bloody and relentless inquisition. Are you willing to join such an organization?

Mar. I am more than willing. I am anxious so to do.

Vic. Will you hold yourself in readiness to join us when called upon?

Mar. Yes.

Vic. [*Both he and Baldwin goes to door,* F.] Then be watchful.

Mar. I have one favor to ask. If I am to join the society of which you have spoken, I would like that my good Bardolf should accompany me. We have been together so long, and he has been so closely allied to my fortunes, that I could not well keep such a secret from him.

Vic. We have trusted you upon your knightly oath. Your esquire is under no such bond.

Mar. I will be answerable for him with my life.

Vic. Then you may broach the secret to him as you please, and if he wishes, he may join with you. It would be well to give him information to-night.

Mar. I will prepare him, sir; and you may rest assured that you will gain a valuable member in him. He has stricken down many an ungodly Moslem. And if need be, he can strike a good blow for liberty of conscience in Germany. Will it be long before we shall be called?

Vic. Not long. We will find you when we are ready, [*Both he and Baldwin, exeunt,* D. F. *Thunder and Lightning.*]

Re-enter BARDOLF, R.

Bard. Then they were not bloody inquisitors.

Mar. Not at all, Bardolf. They were true and worthy knights of the Cross and Sword, and their visit has opened my eyes to something new.

Bard. Ah,——what is it that is new?

Mar. I will tell you, Bardolf, on one condition.

Bard. Name it.

Mar, Not even to save your life will you ever betray your knowledge of this thing to any human being not as justly entitled to that knowledge as you are yourself.

Bard. I give my solemn promise, and swear by the Holy Cross that I'll reveal nothing.

Mar. Now my good Bardolf, I will inform you of the secret. [*both taking seats.*] You have seen those two gentlemen. The elder of the two informed me of the secret, and he calls himself Victor of Antioch, and the younger one calls himself Baldwin of Tyre. The secret is this. There is a society in Germany composed of members of all ages and sex, and the principal thing they are up for is to crush the despised inquisition. The members are Brothers and Friends even to death. And now, Bardolf, do you wish to join such a society of Brothers?

Bard. Will you join, Sir Martin?

Mar. Yes.

Bard. Then I am with you while life lasts! [*Scene closed in.*]

SCENE II.—*A street in Heidelberg.*

Enter MOSES *crying*, L. *and* ANSELMO, R. *meeting.*

Ans. My brother! what is the matter?

Mos. Did you not hear that I was taken last night at twelve o'clock, out of my bed. By the Familiars of the Inquisition. They bound me—gaged me—and dragged me to their Mother,—No, I mean to their Master, the Conrad of Marburg. And he said that I should give my gold, and all my valuables, and if not he would kill me. Of course I did'nt want to give him my valuables, but I had to or else I was afraid of being killed. So I went home and gathered all my Gold and valuables together. But an idea struck me—to run away. I looked out of the window and saw two soldiers watching me. O how bad I felt then. So I went straight back to the Inquisition and I gave all my good things to Conrad—he has got such big eyes, if you would see him, you would be frightened out of your wits,—and then he said that he would give me five days time to leave Baden. O my dear Anselmo, I do not know what to do. I have not ate anything since last night. I have no money—nothing at all, [*crying,*] my poor Gold, [*Flourish of drums and trumpets,* R.] What is that! Ah, soldiers! Come quick! [*both exeunt in a hurry,* L.]

SCENE III.—*Martin Wilsdorf's Apartments. Supper on Table.*

(*See Scene I.*)

BARDOLOF EBERSWALD *discovered seated reading a newspaper.*

Bard. Bless me, why don't he come. It must be past nine o'clock.

Enter KATRINA, R.

Kat. [*as entering,*] Of course it is. The little bit of moon has been down this half-hour. It's past ten, if its anything.

Bard. I'm afraid you are right Katrina. Zounds, I don't like it. There may be something wrong.

Kat. Don't be over anxious, Bardolf. Very likely our master has gone up to the castle. You know the Margrave is his pupil.

Bard. Yes.

Kat. And the prince may have kept him to supper; and so, good Bardolf, you had better eat your own supper; for I can see that you are hungry. You can eat or not, as you choose. I'm well satisfied that Sir Martin has eaten, and I shall clear off the table before I go to bed. [*Exit* R.]

Bard. [*goes to window and looks out.*] Hallo—who is this? [*a knock* D. F.—*opens the door.*]

Enter BALEWIN of Tyre.

Bald. Where is the Saxon Bardolf?

Bard. What do you want with him?

Bald. I have a message for him.

Bard. Then let me have it. I am the man.

Bald. Do you know where your master is.

Bard. No sir.

Bald. Can you not think of something that has kept him out?

Bard. Nothing, sir.

Bald. [*Showing him a ring.*] Do you know what this is?

Bard. [*Looking sharply at it.*] It is my master's signet.

Bald. Certainly. And by this talisman I command you.— You will follow me to the presence of the honorable Knight, Sir Martin Wilsdorf.

Bard. Where is he?

Bald. He is where he needs your company Let that suffice for the present.

Bard. Must I go at once?

Bald. Yes, I await to conduct you.

Bard. [*Anxiously.*] You will please show me the signet once more. [*Baldwin shows the ring to him again—he examines it carefully.*] O yes, that is right—I will just step up stairs and inform our good Katrina—she is our house-keeper—that I am going away. [*Exit R.*]

Re-enter BARDOLF R.

Now sir I am ready to accompany you! [*both exeunt* D. F.]

Scene closed in.

SCENE IV.—*A Street.*

Enter BALDWIN of Tyre and BARDOLF EBERSWALD, L.
Bald. [*Looking without.* R.] Is the noble Knight within.
A Sol. [*Without* R.] He is; and awaits your coming.
Bald. [*to Bardolf.*] You may follow me. [*both exit* R.]

SCENE V.—*A cave occupying the entire stage—a Scaffold,* L.—*door* F.—*a large steel cross and sword,* R.—*four men dressed and masked in black discovered holding a banner representing a cross and sword,* U. C.—*all wear black masks and dominos—four men armed with spears discovered standing* R. *and* L.—*a man is discovered holding a torch at each entrance—*SIR MARTIN WILSDORF, SIR JOSEPH VERDIN, VICTOR OF ANTIOCH, *are disguised standing* L.—*they converse softly together—Bardolf Eberswald discovered bound, his eyes are also bound—stage quite dark—thunder and lightning.*

Ver. Bardolf Eberswald! You may be among friends; and you may be among enemies. Your own answers to our questions will determine. Let him have light! [*A man unties Bardolf's eyes, who is surprised and looks around the stage.*] Bardolf Eberswald, you have been brought hither to give us information, and if you value your life in this world, and your welfare in the world to come, you will answer us without hesitation. Now prepare yourself, and save us from being driven to the use of force. Are you ready to answer?

Bard. Yes, but first I wish you would take this bond from my arms, it pains me.

Ver. Not yet. You will answer a few questions first, and then, if you satisfy us, you shall be free. This slight term of durance will do you no harm. [*Claps with his hands twice—enter two men robed and masked in black bringing a table on which is writing articles and two chairs, R.—and placing them C.—both take seats and writes.*] Now Bardolf Eberswald, you will give me your attention. Have you been in Palestine?

Bard. Yes.

Ver. Who was your master?

Bard. Sir Martin Wilsdorf.

Ver. Do you know if Sir Martin has joined any society since his return from the Holy Land?

Bard. I do not.

Ver. Do you know if he has received any proposition to that end?

Bard. You are going out of your way, sir. If you purpose to question me concerning my master's private affairs, I may as well stop answering at one point as another.

Ver. Do you mean that you will not answer me?

Bard. I mean that it will be entirely useless for you to question me upon any point connected with those affairs of Martin Wilsdorf which belong not to the world.

Ver. I shall question you, nevertheless; and you will be wise if you answer me truly. Now mark: Have you, or have you not heard any allusion made by your master to the existence of a secret organization in Heidelberg?

Bard. I have told you once, and I tell you again, that I will answer no question of that kind. I do not object to this as a single question; but I object to being called upon to disclose any of Sir Martin's secrets.

Ver. Then let me put a question more direct; Have you ever had intimation from any source, that such a society existed in Heidelberg?

Bard. Sir, I know nothing of which you aim, and I have no answer to give. I know not by what authority you question me, and I am not willing to be led into your toils.

Ver. We will see of what stuff you are made, [*Clapping his hands three times—enter two men robed and masked in red—they seize Bardolf—unbind him—and they drag him to the scaffold.*] Once more, Bardolf Eberswald; Will you answer me?

Bard. You have had my answer.

Ver. Hark ye: We are assured that you know of the existence of this secret organization, and we must have your testimony. Will you speak?

Bard. I have spoken!

Ver. Will you die, when a simple answer can save your life!

Bard. [*Pushing the two men away and jumps to the rope.*] I will die before I will prove myself unworthy to live.

Mar. Hold! he has proved himself sufficiently. It is my wish that the ordeal be extended no further. [*Bardolf is surprised at hearing Martin speak and looks anxiously at him.*]

Vic. Right nobly hath he borne the trial. He is worthy to become our brother. [*Martin, Verdin and Victor take off their disguises. Bardolf shakes hands with all.*]

Ver. [*Taking his hand.*] Bardolf Eberswald, surely we cannot hesitate to trust you now; but before we proceed to invest you with our secrets, it becomes necessary that you should take upon yourself a solemn obligation. That obligation Sir Martin has already taken, Have you any objections to take the same?

Bard. I have none.

Scene V.]   THE JEWESS OF HEIDELBERG.   17

Ver. You will follow me. [*leads him to the cross—Bardolf kneels.*] You swear that you will reveal nothing, and be Friends and Brothers with your fellow members even to the death!

Bard. I swear! [*rising.*]

Ver. Remember, should you in the least, by word or deed, violate or transgress any part of this obligation, the dagger of a brother will find your heart. And we are all likewise liable. The meaning of this society is this: Its object is to overthrow the power of the terrible inquisition in Germany; and to the accomplishment of this purpose, every member pledges his life, his fortune, and his sacred honor. If a brother is in distress, you must try and save him with your last drop of blood. And if you wish to know if a man to whom you are speaking, if a Brother or not you do in this way:—First cross yourself, and then if the person is a Brother, he will do in like manner, and answer you in this way: *You are from Antioch?* And your answer:—*From Tyre*—*Your name*—*Henry*—*Is it true?*—*Satisfy yourself*—*The son of God bore a Cross*—*So do I*—*that Cross was of wood*—*mine is of steel*—*So is mine.* Now do you think you will remember the sign?

Bard. Yes sir.

Ver. While you, my brother, hereby pledge your life, if necessary, to serve me, remember that I am bound to you in the same measure; and though I have at present the honor to be Grand Master of the Brotherhood, yet my life is yours should just occasion ever require the sacrifice. [*Takes from pocket a black ribbon on which is suspended a small steel cross pointed like a dagger—ties it around Bardolf's neck.*] And now, in addition to the secrets with which you have been so solemnly entrusted, I hereby invest you with this badge as a mark of your standing in our society. You will wear it always—wear it next your heart—and as you feel it press your bosom, you will be ever reminded of the penalty attached to your obligation.

Bard. I swear once more that I will do my duty as a Brother of this Society. [*Thunder and Lightning.*]

CURTAIN.—END OF ACT I.

ACT II.

SCENE. 1.—*Jacob Olsheim's apartments, richly furnished—table and chairs, c.—A large trunk standing near table which is open, and a number of small bags can be seen in the trunk—books, papers and writing articles is on the table—A door,* F. *and a door leading to a chamber,* R. JACOB OLSHEIM *is discovered walking to and fro.*
The Scene is lighted by a handsome lamp which is on a small table, L.

Enter ELEANOR, R. D.

El. My dear Father, why are you up so late?

Jacob. [*Takes her hand.*] Let me ask you the same question: Why is my Eleanor up so late?

El. Because, I knew that my father was not at rest. Something worries you.

Jacob. How know you that, my child?

El. I can see with my eye of love. I have seen it for some time. I have seen it in your nervous, restless look, and in your unusual depth of thought.

Jacob. You are wonderfully observing, my seraph.

El. Why have you gathered up your jewels, and why have those strong boxes been taken into the vault?

Jacob. Pooh! Don't allow yourself to worry over such things, my child, you don't know half the perplexities of my business.

El. [*looking earnestly into his face.*] My dear father, you entirely misjudge me. I am not the weak woman that can faint and grow powerless in the presence of a danger that can be fully met.

Jacob. Ah, blessed one, you know but little of the dangers that may beset the pathway of earth, my soul! There are dangers so dreadful that even the stoutest man might become as a helpless infant in the presence thereof.

El. Ah, my father, you cannot deceive me; there is some danger. O be sure that this anxiety which is begotten of uncertainty wears more heavily upon me than would any knowledge you could impart. Tell me, I pray you, what we have to apprehend?

Jacob. [*Dropping her hands and turns mournfully away.*] Eleanor, have you ever heard of the Margrave Berthold?

El. [*turning pale.*] Yes, he is ruler in Baden.

Jacob. Aye,——and more powerful in his own dominion than is the emporer. Do you know what manner of a man he is?

El. I have heard that he is a bad man.

Jacob. You have heard the truth, my child. He is a bold, reckless prince, for whom, I verily believe, no work would be too wicked, so that his own selfish ends were answered thereby. And have you ever heard of Conrad of Marburg?

El. Mercy! Let me hope that this terrible man has not turned his evil eye upon us.

Jacob. Alas, my child, I know not in what direction his evil eye may be turned; but I will confess that I do not feel safe in Heidelberg.

El. Is not the emporer your friend?

Jacob. Yes,—he is as much my friend as he can be; but he has litile power in Baden; and moreover, he would not dare to interfere with the officers of the inquisition than he would dare to brave the wrath of Heaven itself.

El. But, do you fear the Inquisition?

Jacob. My dear child, I have reason to fear that terrible power. The inquisition is not only being used for the destruction o heretics, but it has become a vast engine of plunder. I am liable, from two causes, to be brought beneath the fatal torch. I am a Jew, and I am wealthy; and I verily believe that the eyes of both Berthold and Conrad are fixed upon me. I tell you plainly, we must quit Baden. I have already changed most of my gold into rare and costly gems, and as soon as I can make settlement with my friends I shall depart from Heidelberg. Do you remember the rich jeweler Moses?

El. Yes.

Jacob. Do you know where he is?

El. I thought he had left Germany.

Jacob. Alas, Eleanor, I have reason to believe that he has fallen a victim to the demons of the Inquisition.

El. Has he been burned?

Jacob. All victims of the Holy Office are not destroyed by fire. There are other modes of death—modes hidden in deep vaults, far from the light of day, where racks and chains and scourges most dire may eat away human life.

El. Hush, hush, father! O! the God of Israel will not suffer such as us to be thus tortured and murdered.

Jacob. Ah, sweet one, we may not divine the ways of God. Our devoted people have suffered in every land, and what suffering may be in store for us we cannot tell.

El. [*Clinging to him.*] Father! Father! you do not tell me all. You have some cause of fear of which I know not. O hide nothing from me. What is it? What have you discovered?

Jacob. Blessed child, do not be alarmed. I may be over-suspicious. Go to your rest, and sleep away your fears. If there is danger, we may be able to avoid it. I have good friends in Heidelberg, and they will help me if I need help. [*She is about to* speak, but Jacob puts his hand before her mouth.] Say no more to-night, dearest. I have business on my hands which must be attended to before I retire. When the danger comes, be assured you shall know it. God bless you, my child! There—now go.— [*Eleanor exeunt mournfully*, R. D.] Poor child! she does not yet know the full meaning of the cloud that rests over this land. She does not know what a curse my wealth of gold may prove; nor does she dream what a curse her own wealth of beauty may prove to her! [*Sinks on a chair by the table.*] I will hope for the best; and yet I will be prepared for the worst. I know that the eyes of the familiars are upon me; and I believe that the Margrave is leagued with the inquisitior. But I will avoid the shaft if I can. If I am arrested, my doom is certain. The demons will not allow so much wealth to slip through their fingers when so simple and frail a thing as my life stands in the way of the possession. But there is such a thing as disappointment in this world; and, even they may fail in their scheme of plunder. [*Takes bags out of the trunk and places them on the table.*] Poor, worthless baubles! What the apple was to our first mother, thou hast been to all generations!— And the end is not yet. More blood must flow; more human hearts must be crushed; aye, and even empires must be overrun by the sordid avarice which thou canst tempt into the souls of men! But, thanks be to the God of my fathers, I think thou hast led me into no grievous sin, though thou mayest have led me into mortal danger! [*Rising.*] I must put away these harrowing thoughts. [*Goes to the lamp and makes the light quite small— stage dark.*] If I can but sleep a few more nights in safety beneath this roof, all may be well. God help me to escape mine enemies. [*Goes slowly to the* D. F. *but suddenly stops.*] I must not go quite yet. We know not what the morrow may bring forth. It is a dark cloud that overshadows me, and God alone knows when the storm may break. I will make more secure my important papers before I rest. [*Replaces the bags and papers in the trunk. —and then drags the trunk* L. 2 E.—WALTER *and three familiars enter* D. F. *on tip-toe—re-enter* JACOB L. 2 E.—*pale, and goes slowly to* D. F *But is surprised and draws back—Music. Cord.*] What means this! Who are ye?

Wal. We are friends to the just, and enemies to the unjust.

Jacob. And how gained ye admission here?

Wal. Bolts and bars are nothing to us, for all places in Heidelberg are open to us. Jacob Olsheim, you are summoned to appear before a tribunal where justice sits enthroned over the interests of earth and Heaven. Are you prepared?

Jacob. [*Trembling.*] In mercy's name, sir, spare me until the morrow!

Wal. We obey our master.

Jacob. But you will not take me away now!

Wal. That is what we mean to do. [*They seize Jacob, &c. Picture, scene closed in.*]

SCENE II.—*A street.*

Enter ANSELMO, L.

Ans. Thank Heaven I have reached so for. [*falls exhausted,* C] O! ye Gods, how long will I live in this style. [*Looking at his dress.*] this dress—hungry—and no money. No matter that! but as I passed yonder street, I have seen Jacob Olsheim, my poor friend Jacob, thrown into prison just where I escaped from! Tomorrow I was to be brought before the Chief Demon—the Conrad, Ha, ha! but he will be greatly mistaken! [*rising.*] I am hungry: now for Bread, Bread! [*Exeunt,* R.]

SCENE III.—*Prison—a door,* R., *on which is painted a large Red Cross—*JACOB OLSHEIM *is discovered lying chained to a pole. on some straw.* C.

Jacob. Alas! this is the end for me! I need no prophet to open to me the dreadful secret of this place. Had I been less thoughtful of my gold, I might have saved myself. But it is too late now. Oh! my child! my child! What shall become of thee? But I hope that the God of my Fathers may have pity on thee! [*Bell tolls three.*] It is three o'clock. and I am a prisoner in this lonely cell; and in the hands of Conrad of Marburg and Berthold the Margrave of Baden! [*Kneels.*] Father that is in Heaven, have pity on me! King! Maker! and God do have pity on me and on my child, for my poor child's sake. [*Buries his face in his hands and weeps.*]

Enter WALTER *and two familiars.* R. D., *one carrying a torch.*

Wal. [*unbinds Jacob.*] Jacob Olsheim, you will come with us, and you will ask no questions. [*They lift Jacob up who leans on them, and all exeuent,* R. D.]

SCENE IV.—*Plain Chamber.*

Enter HECTOR, L.

Hec. [*Thoughtfully.*] What, Jacob Olsheim, the rich Jew—my old and kind friend, is in the hands of Conrad and Berthold—then he is a dead man. They will slay him; not because he is a Jew, but because he is rich and wealthy. I would like to save him, but as I cannot, I will try and save his daughter! [*exit* R.]

SCENE V.—*Chambers of the Inquisition—Four Familiars,* R.—*Armed with spears—*BERTHOLD *the Mangrave is discovered seated on a Throne,* U. C.—*three soldiers are standing each side of him—Four Familiars,* L. *armed with spears—they leave a space between them so as to leave people pass in and out—*CONRAD *of Marburg is discovered seated in front of a familiar,* R. 4, E.—*two Familiars are discovered seated at a table,* C. *writing—*JACOB OLSHEIM *is also discovered standing looking pale, &c.,* L.

Stage gradually dark.

Con. Jacob Olsheim, do you know where you are?

Jabob. I think I do.

Con. And whither does your thought lead you?

Jacob. To the Inquisition.

Con. You have rightly judged. You are in the torture-chamber of the Holy Office, and you will be wise if you answer such questions as may be asked, with truth and promptness. First, I will ask you—what is your religious faith?

Jacob. I am a Jew.

Con. Have you ever bowed to the Cross of Christ?

Jacob. I have never worshipped Jesus of Nazareth, though I have——

Con. Hold! You will answer without explanation. If you are a Jew, and have never worshipped at the foot of the cross, then your influence has been against God's holy church.

Jacob. Not so. No man in the Empire has done more towards helping the soldiers of the cross against the Saracen than I have done. My gold helped Henry with his armament; and Frederic owed much of his success to my aid.

Con. And what was your aim in this?

Jacob. I have never demanded unjust usury.

Con. What care we for your usury. You had a deeper scheme than that. We verily believe that it has been your earnest desire to see the Saracen swept from the Holy Land; but the end you had in view was not a righteous one. You did not mean that the cross of Christ should be established in Palestine. You had planned that the Saracen should be swept away, and then you hoped that the Jews, gathering from all quarters of the world, might, in time, sweep away the remnant of the Christian army, and thus possess themselves of the land from which an outraged God had driven them. Am I not right?

Jacob. No, no. Such a thought never entered my head.

Con. Beware, Jacob Olsheim! Falsehood cannot serve you. Answer me truly: is there not to-day in Germany, a secret society of Jews, pledged to the accomplishment of this purpose?

Jacob. What purpose?

Con. The purpose of establishing the Israelitish power once more in the Holy Land.

Jacob. No, no. I know there is no such society.

Con. How do you know?

Jabob. I know that the Jews have no design to possess themselves of the old heritage by force.

Con. And you think they have no hopes of ever regaining the Kingdom which their fathers lost.

Jacob. I will not speak a falsehood. The scattered tribes of Israel do hope that in time to come, God will raise up a Prince under whose reign the glory of David's Kingdom shall be restored.

Con. Aye, and people who cherish such hopes will naturally bend their energies towards realizing them. And now sir, who is at the head of this Society of Jews in Baden?

Jacob. I know of no such society.

Con. Where are the meetings held in Heidelberg?

Jacob. I know of no meetings of the kind.

Con. Jacob Olsheim, there is such a society in existence, the aim of which is to return the Holy Land to the darkness of Judaism; and that society has a branch in Baden; and we are furthermore persuaded that no Jew has been left in ignorance thereof.— Once more I ask you: who is at the head of this society in Baden?

Jacob. As God is my judge, I know nothing of it.

Con. Know ye, vile Jew, that God doth not always judge men by his own direct power. He hath appointed his ministers of justice, and to them must your appeal be made. That which the sinner will not confess willingly, may be drawn from him by other means. [*Claps with his hands once. Bell tolls one.*]

Enter WALTER *and* 1 *Familiar,* L.—*they seize Jacob.*
Jacob Olsheim, you have one more opportunity to speak of your own free will. What know you of the society of which I have spoken?

Jacob. I know nothing. [*Bell tolls two. Walter and the Familiar seize and drag Jacob to the* L. E.]

Con. [*Looking to the left.*] You have my question, and you can answer when you please. [*the noise of rattling with chains is heard,* L.]

Jacob. [*Groaning without,* L.] I know nothing. I know nothing.]

Wal. [*without*] He has fainted.

Ber. Be careful! He must not die yet. We must know where his wealth is stored.

Con. Fear not. He has not approached the gates of death. We will give him back his senses, and try a new motive. [*raises from his seat and goes to the* L. *looking in.*] Walter, unloosen those chains a little. [*a pause. The noise of chains is heard again.*] Jacob Olsheim, the place where you now rest will be your place of death if you do not answer me promptly and truly. You have much wealth?

Jacob. [*Faintly.*] Yes.

Con. Before we proceed to more important subjects we would know where your wealth is to be found. Will you tell us? [*A pause.*] Jacob Olsheim, where is your gold?

Jacob. It is where I hope you may never find it.

Con. Fool! Will you sacrifice your life to save your gold? [*the noise is heard again.*] Where is your gold? [*a groan is heard.*] Will you not answer? [*The noise of chains is still heard.*] Will you answer now? [*stamping his foot.*]

Ber. [*starting forward.*] Hold! hold! The man must not be killed yet!

Wal. [*without,* L.] I fear you are too late! that sign is fatal.

Con. He was weaker than I had thought. Ease down the pulleys quickly, and let us see if there is any life left. [*both he and Berthold exit in a hurry. Scene closed in.*]

SCENE VI.—*A Plain Room—a table and two chairs carried in by the servant—wine and tumblers are on table.*

Enter CONRAD *of Marburg and* BERTHOLD *the Mangrave.* L.

Con. I am sorry that the Jew dropped off so quickly. [*both take seats.*]

Ber. So am I. But we may have lost nothing. A careful search of the old heretic's house may reveal to us his wealth. [*both drink.*]

Con. We may make another arrest first. The old man has left a daughter behind him.

Bar. Aye! and by Saint Paul, she is the most beautiful damsel in all Baden. In this case, Conrad, you must allow me to make division of the spoils. You may set your own price upon the maiden, but you must give her up to me.

Con. Ah, my lord, [*laughing,*] have you found another heart-prize?

Ber. Yes,—I freely confess it. I saw the Jewess not long since, and I swear to you, she is past all power of mine to fittingly describe. She must be mine. Do not say me nay.

Con. Indeed, my prince, if you want the damsel you may have her; but you had better let my familiars arrest her. Let her be brought hither and questioned, and she shall then be delivered over to you.

Ber. And what will you gain from her by questioning?

Con. Something, perhaps, concerning her father's wealth. These old Jews are notorious for craftily concealing their gold. Do you remember David, the usurer? I am convinced that we did not find a third part of his hidden store.

Ber. It may be as you say, but the girl must not be put to the torture. By the mass, I would not have her sweet form distorted for all the gold her father ever owned. Will you promise me this?

Con. It shall be as you wish, my lord. If you have set your heart upon the possession of the beautiful Jewess, she shall be yours, and no touch of our executioners shall mar her loveliness of form or feature.

Ber. Then let her be brought hither at once. You shall question her to-day, and to-night, under cover of the darkness I will bear her to my castle. Shall it be so?

Con. Yes.

Ber. And you will send true and trusty men?

Con. I have none others.

Ber. I mean men who will not make too free with the maiden; for, as true as I live, she hath gained entire possession of my heart. [*both drink and rise.*]

Con. Fear not my lord. My familiars will watch each other so your sweet prize will be safe. But, after all, it may puzzle you to tame her. These Jewish daughters are not easily won by such as us.

Ber. Leave that to me. She may choose as she pleases—there are other persuasive racks beside those in your torture-chamber!

Con. Now, my good Prince, we will send for the beautiful Jewess. [*both exit, L.*]

Scene VII.—*Martin Wilsdorf's Apartments*—Sir Martin Wilsdorf *discovered shutting the door, F. as scene opens.*

Mar. My pupils have gone, and—[*a knock, D. F.*] Ah! somebody knocking; come in.

     Enter Victor of Antioch.

Vic. Are you alone?

Mar. Aye, my brother; only Bardolf and myself are here.

Vic. This is a late visit, but a matter of business demands our attention. I trust you are ready for work.

Mar For any good work I am always ready.

Vic. And be assured, that I shall never call upon you for any other. You know Jacob Olsheim, the rich Jew?

Mar. I have seen him.

Vic. Do you know his dwelling place?

Mar. Yes.

Vic. The Jew is, of course, not a member of our brotherhood; but he is nevertheless a valuable friend, and we owe him much not only so, but we may need his assistance in the time to come Nor is this all. Olsheim is not a marked victim of the inquisition. Conrad of Marburg and the Margrave of Baden have their eyes upon his great wealth; and we have reason to believe that they will endeavor soon to arrest him. He must be saved, and to you the task is given. Will you accept it?

Mar. Aye, right gladly. Jacob Olsheim was a true friend to my father. I remember once that he lent him two thousand double ducats of gold, and the only security which he demanded was my father's pledge of honor.

Vic. Such is the character of the man. And we must save him. You can go to his dwelling early in the morning and bring him hither; and beyond that we can keep him as may seem best. He has a daughter, I am told, and she too, must be saved. Let her accompany her father. Baldwin of Tyre and myself start for Mannheim within an hour, and we shall not return until to-morrow evening.

Mar. You are sure that the demons intend to arrest the Jew?

Vic. Yes. We have a brother within the walls of the inquisition, and he has brought to me the intelligence that Olsheim's name is upon their fatal list. Remember, Wilsdorf, the man of wealth who once passes the threshold of the Holy Office, never comes forth alive.

Mar. Might it not be better to bring the Jew hither this very night?

Vic. I think not. The familiars of the inquisition are abroad by night, and they might detect the movement. It is now near midnight, and the Jew could not be aroused without some disturbance, as the outer gate is kept firmly locked. There can be no danger attending the task, unless, indeed, the daughter should prove to be young and beautiful.

Mar. I have little to fear from the beauty of a Jewess.

Vic. I don't know about that. I have heard that this Jewess is both young and lovely; and if such is the fact, I should judge from what I know of her father, that she would be pure-minded and modest, possessing all those virtues which go to make up the perfect woman. But perhaps you already have a fair lady-love.

Mar. No, my brother; I am not so encumbered; nor am I anxious to venture upon the erotic sea at present. I can save both the Jew and his daughter without heart danger to myself.

Vic. Then be at work early in the morning, for Jacob is not apt to oversleep himself if he is at all like others of his people whom I have known. [*exit D. F.*]

Mar. [*Goes to door.*] Yes, my brother, I will be there early to-morrow, without fail. [*Scene closed in.*]

Scene VIII.—*A Street in Heidelberg.*

Enter Sir Martin Wilsdorf, r., *and* Hector, l., *meeting.*

Mar. Who art thou?

Hec. Who art thou?

Mar. I am going on honest business. Can you say the same?

Hec. I can say more than that, I have come through a most perilous way to reach this street. Can you say the same? [*Hector* makes the sign of a cross on his breast—*Martin sees it and does the same.*] Ah! You are from Antioch?

Mar. From Tyre!
Hec. Your name?
Mar. Henry.
Hec. Is it true?
Mar. Satisfy yourself,
Hec. The Son of God wore a cross.
Mar. So do I.
Hec. That cross was of wood.
Mar. Mine is of Steel.
Hec. So is mine. [*shaking hands together.*] And we are brothers well met. Now, whence come you and what is your business?

Mar. I come from Victor of Antioch, and my business is to save the Jew and his daughter.

Hec. You are too late to save the Jew. He is past all human help.

Mar. Ha! Victor told me that we had a brother within the walls,——

Hec. Enough! I am the man, and it was I who bore the intelligence of the Jew's danger to him of Antioch. But the familiars have been before you. I did not give the notice soon enough. Olsheim was taken hence last night.

Mar. And where is he now?
Hec. Dead.
Mar. Ha!——

Hec. But it is not too late to save the child. I had come for the purpose of warning her away; but you can do more. You can do both—warn her and give her safe conduct; only, my brother, you must make haste. The order has been already issued for her arrest, and the familiars may soon be here. I think you know your duty if you meet them.

Mar. My duty is to obey the orders of my chief.

Hec. At all hazards!

Mar. I understand you.

Hec. Then hasten on. Know that Jacob Olsheim died upon the rack this very morning; and the daughter, if she is arrested, is doomed to a worse fate.

Mar. A worse?

Hec. Aye. She has to live!

Mar. What! Live! Ah, I understand all. [*both shake hands together.*] Once more, my brother, I swear I will try and save her. So farewell. [*exeunt* MARTIN L. *and* HECTOR R.]

SCENE IX.—JACOB OLSHEIM'S *apartments.*
(*See Scene* I. *in Act* II.)
CALYPSO *discovered seated* C.
Enter WILSDORF D. F.

Mar. My good woman, time is precious. I am a friend to be trusted. If your master is not in I must see your mistress. Stop not to question me, but go instantly and arouse the lady. [*Exit* CALYPSO R. D.]

Enter ELEANOR R. D.

El. Did you wish to see me, sir?

Mar. Are you the daughter of Jacob Olsheim?

El. I am, sir.

Mar. Lady, time is precious, and I must speak briefly and to the point. I am not used to wandering around a subject when I find a strange path leading directly to it. Do you know where your father is?

El. Do you know where he is? [*Martin hesitates.*] Remember, sir, you said you would speak plainly. O, I see it in your face! Some evil hath befallen him!

Mar. Yes, lady. And the same evil which hath befallen him will surely befall you if you remain longer beneath this roof.—Listen to me, and I will tell you the whole truth. [*Eleanor takes a seat.*] You have true friends in Heidelberg. Last night I was waited upon by one of those friends, and by him instructed to come hither this morning and lead Jacob Olsheim and his daughter hence to a place of safety, for it was known that a great evil threatened him.

El. And that evil was from the dreadful Inquisition?

Mar. You are right, lady.

El. [*She weeps, &c.*] O! I feared it! My father feared it! God have mercy on us!

Mar. Gentle lady, you know not what pain it gives me to proceed; but you must know the worst.

El. Noble sir, I pray you conceal nothing. Let me know all.

Mar. This morning, I came here as directed, and as I entered the court, I was accosted by a stranger, whom I afterwards found to be a brother. He had come with a message to you—to warn you to flee instantly from this house. Your father was arrested by the familiars of the Inquisition last night. And an order has been issued for your arrest.

El. [*Rising.*] Kind sir, you are my friend.

Mar. Yes, lady; and I have good reason for it. Your father was one of the truest friends my father ever had. Did you ever hear the name of Joseph Wilsdorf?

El. Yes, sir—a brave Christian Knight, whom my father equipped for battle.

Mar. The same, lady; and I am the son of that Joseph Wilsdorf; and I, too, am a Christian Knight; my name is Martin. I think you will trust me.

El. Yes, yes,—and you will tell me the truth. My father is doomed to die? [*Martin is silent and tears start in his eyes.*]— My father is dead!

Mar. He is dead!

El. [*Clasping her hands together in agony.*] Then—then, let me go and die with him!

Mar. Alas, gentle lady, that may not be. Your father died, not because he was a Jew, but because he was wealthy. If the fair daughter falls into those fatal hands, she will not suffer as her father suffered.

El. Why should they spare me?

Mar. They would spare you for a fate far worse!

El. Worse!

Mar. Yes—a thousand times. O, sweet lady, you must linger here no longer. The messenger who told me of your father's death, knew what would be your fate. Shall I translate his meaning for your ears?

El. Tell me the truth.

Mar. I think the castle of Heidelberg is meant for the scene of your torture!

El. Merciful God!

Mar. Berthold of Baden is a villian of the darkest dye.

Enter 2 FAMILIARS, D. F.—*They stand there.*

And he rules with Conrad of Marburg over the iniquities of the Inquisition. [*He is surprised at seeing the familiars.*] Ha! Whom have we here? By the Holy Cross, they are upon us!

El. O! kind sir, in God's name, save me!

Mar. While I live you are safe. These men shall not harm you.

1*st Fam.* We seek the Jewess Eleanor, daughter of Jacob Olsheim.

Mar. The lady is here, and I am here to answer for her.

1*st Fam.* You will answer when you are called upon. And

that may be much sooner than you expect. I know you sir, and if I once whisper your name within the walls of our office, Martin Wilsdorf will have need of more help than yonder Jewess is likely at present to find! Stand aside, and let the daughter of Olsheim speak for herself.

Mar. One moment, sirs, if you please, before you proceed further, let me enlighten you. I am this lady's guardian, and I shall defend her with my life.

1st Fam. Do you know who we are?

Mar. I think I do.

1st Fam. Do you know the nature of our office?

Mar. Unless I am greatly mistaken, you are familiars of the Inquisition.

1st Fam. You are right. We are from the Holy Office, and we come hither with authority. We will not arrest you now, but if you are wise you will take yourself out of our way as quickly as possible.

Mar. Gentlemen, you do not understand me, it is you who had better take yourselves off, for by the powers of Heaven I swear, you shall not lay a hand on this lady. [*the familiars start.*] Hold, let me finish, for I would have you know the grounds of my action. The lady's father is dead.—

1st Fam. Ha! How know you that?

Mar. I know it by the astonishment you now express. You are not good at keeping secrets! And now let me tell you one thing more: If this fair lady is taken to your black-hearted master, her fate will be worse than has been her father's. [*The familiars converse together and then both draw their swords.*]

1st Fam. Martin Wilsdorf, your execution will come first and your trial afterwards. This is the fate of those who dare to oppose the holy authority of the inquisition! [*Martin also draws his sword.*]

El. [*catching Martin by the arm.*] No, no!—not for me!

Mar. Hush, lady, you had far better die where you stand than fall into the hands of these men. Remember my oath! [*he pushes Eleanor away, who falls on a seat and covers her face with her hands and weeps.* Now you can attack me if you dare; for you touch not that lady while I stand here. I know you well, and before God I feel assured that the just spirits of Heaven would approve the stroke that reached your dastard hearts. You are not officers of a proper court—you are not ministers of any Christian law, but you are attendant demons upon a foul institution, whose only office is murder and robbery! In all the broad spread of heathen lands, there is nothing so wicked as is your deadly inquisition; and among all the tyrants of the earth the eye of the avenging angel rests not upon one so deeply steeped in bloody guilt as is your chief! Now we know each other, and you may understand how fearlessly I will raise my hand against you! [*Alarums—they fight—both familiars fall.*] Come, there must be no moment lost. This roof can no longer give you safe shelter!

El. Where are those dark men? I heard a fall—a groan—Oh—.

Mar. Look not that way, lady; look upon me and come.

El. Are they both dead?

Mar. They are both beyond the power of doing you harm; but there are others where they came from, and some of these others may soon be here. Collect what you wish to take with you as speedily as possible.

El. Calypso must go with me, kind sir.

Mar. Do you speak of the old domestic I saw when I came in?

El. Yes.

Mar. She may go with us, but bid her move quickly. [*exit Eleanor, R. D.—he gazes on the bodies of the familiars.*] I know not whether I ought to be sorry for this or not. Still, I did what I was forced to do. And, by Saint Paul, I'd sooner dip my sword in the blood of the whole army of inquisitors and familiars than that mortal harm should come through them to this lovely maid. Well shall it be for Germany when the demons are all swept away.

Re-enter ELEANOR *and* CALYPSO, R. D., *closely veiled.*
Are you ready?
El. I am. [*Music—all exeunt,* D. F.

SCENE X.—*A Street in Heidelberg.*
Music—Enter SIR MARTIN WILSDORF, ELEANOR *aud* CALYPSO *in a hurry,* L.
Mar. Yonder house, dear lady, is my dwelling, and I hope it will be a place where you can stay and escape danger for the present. [*All exit,* R.]

SCENE XI.—*Martin Wilsdorf's Apartments.*
Enter WILSDORF, ELEANOR *and* CALYPSO, D. F.
Mar. [*taking Eleanor's hand.*] Lady, I know how sad and heavy is the blow which has fallen upon you, and I know how your orphaned spirit must grieve; but let me hope that you will find some slight consolation in the fact of your own salvation from a dreadful doom, and that the knowledge that you have good and true friends may cause you to feel some slight disposition to raise the heart in gratitude to the Father of mercies. For the present you will be safe here, and I beg that you will make known your every wish. You have but to command me while you are under my protection.
El. And shall I have to leave you?
Mar. My first and highest aim, dear lady, is your safety; and, be it here, or be it elsewhere, my interest in your welfare shall not cease. Ah! here comes my good Katrina.

Enter KATRINA, R.

Go with her, and she will provide for you. [*exit all* R. *except Martin.*]

Enter BARDOLF EBERSWALD, R.

Bard. I am indeed glad, Sir Martin, that you have safely returned and brought the Jewess with you. But why is her father not here?

Mar. Her father, poor man, is already dead; the familiars of the inquisition arrested him last night. But, I tell you, Bardolf, I had quite a trouble in getting his daughter here. I have killed two familiars!

Bard. How was that?

Mar. [*takes a seat.*] When I left here this morning, I was met by a stranger—who afterwards proved to be a brother, and he informed me of the death of Jacob Olsheim, and that an order had been issued for the arrest of his daughter. What do you think her fate would be?

Bard. I suppose the same as was her fathers.

Mar. Worse!

Bard. What! worse! how can that be! [*Martin whispers in his ear.*] Mercy! But how came you to kill the familiars?

Mar. As I was speaking to the Jewess, the two familiars made their appearance and demanded her. But I did not let them have her, so they drew their swords and wanted to take us both. But I made quick work with them!

Bard. I hope you were not observed! What would your life be worth?

Mar. It would be worth but little, I confess, should I fall into the clutches of the inquisition; but I do not mean that shall be the case; And now Bardolf you must go into the street in which stands the Jew's house, and observe what happens. You know what I want, [*exit,* R.]

Bard. O! yes, my master, I understand you well enough.
[*Exit* D. F.]

Scene XII.—*A Street in Heidelberg.*
Enter Bardolf Ederswald, R.

Bard. Just yonder is the house,—to-day I must keep my eyes and ears open, for my good master will like to hear of something new. Why, as I live, some body is down there. But I will see what he is doing there. [*Exit* L.]

Scene XIII.—*A Plain Chamber.* Berthold *discovered walking to and fro.*
Enter Conrad of Marburg, R.

Ber. How now, Conrad,—have those familiars returned?

Con. No, my lord; and I am at a loss to account for their delay.

Ber. It must be that the girl has fled. By heaven, I'd rather lose half my dominions than lose her. She must be mine. I have set all my hopes upon the possession. Good Conrad, let other messengers be sent. Gain her for me, and you may claim all her dead father's gold.

Con. You shall have her, my lord. I'll send other officers directly. [*Calling.*] Walter.
Enter Walter, R.

You must immediately go to the Jews house, and see what is the matter with our two familiars. And also bring the Jews daughter with you. Be quick, and return as soon as possible. [Walter *exit* R.—*both he and* Berthold *converse together.*]
Enter Therwald, R.

Ther. [*to* Conrad.] Anselmo cannot be found.

Con. How far have you been.

Ther. As far as Ulm.

Con. Well, you take a few men with you, and go to Mannheim, and if you can't find him, return and I will give you further instructions. [THERWALD *exit* R.—*they converse together.*]

Re-enter WALTER, R., *pale.*

How is it, Walter. Where are the others?

Wal. [*Crossing himself.*] God save us, my master!

Ber. Speak out. This matter is no secret from me.

Con. Speak.

Wal. Satan is let loose! We went to the house of the Jew, and we found no living thing within its walls; but we found our two brothers cold and dead!

Ber. How! dead?

Wal. Yes, even so!

Ber. And in the Jew's house?

Wal. Yes. One of them had his head split open and the other had been stabbed to the heart. The work must have been done by a strong arm.

Ber. Aye, and the arm must have been guided by one well use to handling the sword. Good Heavens, Conrad, what shall we do?

Con. Walter, do you mean that both the familiars have been murdered?

Wal. Yes.

Con. Did you learn anything further?

Wal. No. We chose not to make inquiries of outsiders.

Con. [*to Berthold.*] Then first we will go with a trusty force and search the old Jew's house. We can find his gold, and we may find some clue to this fearful mystery.

Ber. But the girl. What of her? Remember there is more than the old man's gold to be found.

Con. She shall be searched for, my lord; and she shall be found too. And when we have found her, we will find who did this deed of blood. Fear not; for I swear to you that not in all

Baden can my once marked victim be hidden from me. You shall have the lovely Jewess, and I will have the man or the men whose hands have shed this blood! [*all exeunt,* R]

Scene XIV.—*A Street in Heidelberg.*
Flourish of Trumpets and Drums—Enter Conrad *of Marburg,* Berthold, Walter, *two Soldiers and four Familiars,* R. *all go across the stage and exit,* L.

Scene XV.—*Jacob Olsheim's Apartments.*
The two familiars are discovered lying on the floor—as dead.
Enter Conrad, Berthold Walter, *two Soldiers and four familiars,* D. F.

Ber. Ah! There they are!

Con. [*Both he and Berthold examine the bodies.*] The first thing to do is to lay aside these corses, and the next will be to clean the house of its wealth. This matter shall be attended to in due time. Now my men, to work! and let us raze this house to the ground. [*He sends the familiars in different directions—the two soldiers carry the bodies through* D. F. *Walter looks all over the stage and overturns everything—he exits,* R. D. *Conrad and Berthold converse together—the noise of breaking of boxes is heard from all parts of the stage—the noise suddenly stops—Re-enter four familiars, the two soldiers and Walter, bringing a small box.*]

Wal. [*to Conrad.*] Here my master, is a box I have found.

Con. [*taking the box.*] So, so, Jacob, you did not think that I was so smart as to find your gold! [*opens the box and counts.*] Only one thousand ducats? Holy Saint Peter! We cannot have been so deceived. The wretch had more wealth. This paltry sum could not purchase a single one of the rare gems I have seen him wear upon his finger.

Ber. Down with the building! and thus the workmen may

bring the hidden store to light. [*he sends the soldiers,* R. D. *and Conrad sends the familiars in different parts—A Red flame is seen in* R. D. *leading to the chamber, Walter rushes out.*] Ah! The house is burning! [*both he and Conrad rush out,* D. F.—*the interior of the house falls and is on fire—Picture.*]

CURTAIN.—END OF ACT II.

ACT III.

SCENE I.—*Martin Wilsdorf's Apartments.*
ELEANOR *is discovered sitting on a chair.*
Enter BARDOLF EBERSWALD, D. F.

El. Good Bardolf, you have just come from my home?
Enter SIR MARTIN WILSDORF, R.
You will please let me hear what Bardolf has to say, you will, will you not?

Mar. O, yes, sweet lady. Now Bardolf, tell us what you have seen and heard.

Bard. After I left here I came to your father's house, and then I went into the garden and seated myself behind a bush, where I could easily see and hear what was going on. I did not wait long when two familiars came and went into the house—and by the way they were speaking; they were greatly surprised in finding two of their companions dead. They searched the house and then went away. In a short time afterwards those two returned with Conrad and Berthold, and with many of their attendants. I heard the chief demon swear that he must have you, and he must have the man or the men who killed those two familiars; and they all commenced to break up the chests and doors, and in fact everything that they could get a hold of.

Mar. Ah, they were after their victim's gold.

Bard. Certainly. But I don't believe they found much of it. At all events, they came forth in anything but a satisfied mood, and I am sure that I heard both Conrad and Berthold curse and swear most profanely.

Mar. [*to Eleanor.*] Lady, what think you, did your father have much wealth in his house?

El. I think he did sir, but I doubt if those men were able to find it. They may have found some gold, but my father's chief wealth was not in that cumbersome shape.

Bard. Yes, I think they found something of value, for I noticed a man carry a small box with him. But the place is desolate enough now; after they had searched for the gold, a demon crew came and razed the house to the ground, so that now there is not left a stick nor a stone above the foundation. But, my master, this is not all; the spies of the inquisition are posted in every quarter of the city, and the avenues of egress are all guarded. The Margrave's soldiers guard the gates while the spies prowl through the streets.

El. [*trembling.*] Does that mean me?

Bard. Yes, lady. They are all well satisfied that they have not found the bulk of your father's wealth, and they think if they can but get the daughter into their power, the secret may be opened to them. But that is not the worst. Ah, no! let me assure you that your father's gold is not all!

Mar. How know you this?

Bard. I'll tell you bye and bye.

Mar. [*to Eleanor.*] Dear lady, you are safe here for the present, so let not this account give you new trouble. Before I retire I will take measures to satisfy myself as to whether any suspicion turns this way. Go now and make yourself as comfortable as possible, and believe that you have friends who will allow no further harm to befall you if it is in their power to prevent.

El. Indeed sir, you are very kind, and I hope Heaven will reward you.

Mar. [*taking her hand.*] Heaven can give me no greater reward than your gratitude. You would hardly feel safe beneath the protection of one who expected reward for those services which the true knight ever renders to suffering humanity, in simple obedience to the call of duty. The reward which I claim lady, is the approval of my own conscience; but I cannot hide from you that your sweet gratitude will give me much joy; and I could know that I was remembered in the prayers of one so pure and good, the reflection would be grateful beyond measure.

El. Ah, kind sir, you forgot that I am a Jewess. What can the Christian need of prayers to the God of the Jews?

Mar. It is you who forget. The God of Abraham, Isaac and Jacob—the God who led his chosen people Israel out from bondage—is the God I worship. He is to me as he is to you, the one Living and True God. Am I not right?

El. Yes, kind sir.

Mar. Then pray for me; and if the thought should force itself upon you that the Jews have no part with Christians, remember that the demons against whom my hand is now turned in your behalf, call themselves Christians. The Great Teacher whose lessons of life I would be glad to follow, has told us: Blessed are the pure in heart, for they shall see God. And it is not for me, lady, to say that the sons and daughters of the people whom God once loved, may not even now, enjoy the warm bright smiles of Heaven, if they are pure in heart.

El. When I pray, I shall not forget you. [*exit,* R.]

Bard. Now, my master—.

Mar. Yes, yes, Bardolf, you were saying that you knew more than you had told.

Bard. More than I could speak in the hearing of the lady. On my way from the scene of the ruin, I was overtaken by a man who proved himself to be a Brother. He said he saw you this morning. Do you remember him?

Mar. Aye, very well.

Bard. He told me that strict search was being made for the daughter of Jacob Olsheim, and that the city would be searched from end to end. They did not find much money in the old Jew's house, and they think the daughter can tell where to look. But this is not all. The wicked Margrave has an interest in the matter.

Mar. I understand. O, I know the disposition of that titled wretch, but he cannot succeed, I will defend the maiden with my life. They may—— [*A. knock*, D. F.] It is Victor of Antioch. Go and admit him. [*Bardolf opens the door.*]

Enter HECTOR, D. F.

Hec. Martin Wilsdorf, I will enter your house, for I have something to say to you.

Mar. My brother, you can speak my name; and you can also speak the name of this member of our fraternity, but we cannot thus designate yourself.

Hec. You may call me Hector, and you will bear in mind that I have need of the utmost caution, for I have to serve in a double capacity. Conrad of Marburg thinks I serve him, and he must not be undeceived at present.

Mar. Truly not. But tell me, if you have the right—Are you the only one of our Brotherhood that wears the robes of the holy office?

Hec. I am the only one in Heidelberg, though I hope I may have companionship ere long. But we must not waste time now. The daughter of the Jew is at this moment beneath your roof.— [*Martin hesitates.*] My brother, you must be frank with me; for I am risking more than life in thus calling upon you.

Mar. Pardon me. I did but follow an inclination born of caution. The daughter of Jacob Olsheim is beneath my roof.

Hec. Then you must contrive some way to shield her for this night. Your house will be searched within an hour.

Mar. How!

Burd. This house searched!

Hec. Yes. Every house in Heidelberg will be searched before the work is abandoned, and yours come among the first, as this street is in one of the districts that will be visited to-night.

Mar. And do they suspect me?

Hec. No. They suspect no one yet; but it is known that the girl must be in the city, and consequently, no dwelling will be left unsearched.

Mar. By the mass, this is most unfortunate! Whither can I convey her?

Hec. She must not be taken hence to-night, Sir Martin, for there are spies at every turn, and no person can pass unchallenged. To move her beyond these walls at present would be both fatal to her and yourself. You must contrive some way to shield her.

Mar. Mercy! I know of no secure hiding-place within these walls. I can but defend her with my good sword.

Hec. Ah, you must not think of that. Set your wits at work, and see if you cannot contrive some quiet way of avoiding detection. On the morrow the girl may be removed, should it be deemed necessary. It is unfortunate for us that we thus have her upon our hands. The aim of our Grand Master was, to save her father; but as he is gone, and his child has fallen into our hands, we cannot desert her. And, furthermore, her arrest now would be dangerous to ourselves, for there is no telling what the inquisitors might extort from her.

Mar. [*Thinking.*] Are you sure that no suspicion is turned this way?

Hec. Certainly I am. Holy Mother! Had there been a suspicion ever so slight of that sort, your dwelling would not have remained unvisited thus long. But my brother, I must leave the work with you. The spies and familiars must be near at hand and not for my life would I be found here. I can help you no farther. You know what is coming, and you must prepare to meet it. Only, let me call your attention to one fact: the eyes of these wolves are sharp, and their scent is keen. No ordinary hiding-place will escape their observation.

Mar. Within an hour, you say, they will be here?

Hec. It cannot be much longer.

Mar. I will do the best I can.

Bard. [*Crossing himself.*] And may God help us.

Hec. [*He goes to door F., and suddenly stops.*] I must not leave the matter in this way. [*He goes to the table and takes from his pocket a paper—it contains red powder—and pours some into another paper and gives it to Martin.*] Sir Martin, we must not forget the sacred compact into which we have voluntarily entered; nor must we forget that the end we have in view is the salvation of an empire. The Jewess may be taken; but, if we can prevent it, she must not go alive into the hands of the inquisitiors Do not start. Even for her own sake, this simple powder would be as an angel of mercy; for she had better die within the hour of her purity, than become the victim of the black-hearted Berthold. But there is a consideration beyond this; she is a weak woman, and in her terror she would be almost sure to reveal all that she knew.

Mar. And what does she know?

Hec. She knows that you slew the two familiars. She could give them a clue, and when the demons have once gained that they will know which way to turn. Take this powder and mix it with wine, or with water, in a cup; and if, in the last extremity, you find that the girl must fall into the hands of the familiars of the inquisition, you will cause her to drink the potion. Be assured, my brother, it will be better so for us, and better for her. [*Martin takes the powder.*]

Mar. Just heaven! Do you think I can thus become the murderer of——

Hec. Hold! You will be her deliverer—not her murderer.—Should I command you to do this, you could not escape the work.

Mar. Ha! You command? [*Hector throws open his coat and shows on his vest a steel cross surmounted by an eagle.*]—You are our lieutenant.

Hec. I am. And now remember my instructions. Let not the beauty of the maiden unnerve your arm in the hour of a nation's peril. One false step now—one unfortunate discovery of our existence—might prove fatal to the high hopes of thousands. You understand me. [*Exit* D. F.]

Bard. It is the lieutenant. He is next in power to the grand master himself.

Mar. Yes.

Bard. And his commands must be obeyed, when given under the signet of his high office.

Mar. By the Holy Angels! The maiden shall not die. Good Heaven! Sooner will I take the fatal potion!

Bard. Easy. The only thing to be benefitted by your death, would be the abominable inquisition. But, my master, let us reason calmly. Can we not save the lady?

Mar. Save her. How?

Bard. By hiding her.

Mar. Alas, we have no place beneath this roof.

Bard. Perhaps we may find a place.

Mar. Bardolf, if you can find a place, you shall have my eternal gratitude.

Bard. She must be hidden in the simplest and boldest manner. Bolts and bars, and secret closets, and deep vaults could be of no avail, for the villians know how to overcome all such objects.— Leave it to me, and I will so conceal her that she shall not be discovered.

Mar. And how will you do it?

Bard. By placing her where she will be the first person seen by the spies.

Mar. I do not understand you.

Bard. Send for the lady, and make her acquainted with the necessity, and then we will see how far she can help herself. We must be expeditious, for the rascals may be along very soon. [*Martin exit* R, *and re-enter conversing with Eleanor,* R.] If you have the courage and nerve to act the part I am able to give you, I feel I can answer for your safety.

El. Anything! Anything! I can be strong in such an extremety.

Bard. Then come with me, and take heart, Katrina shall help us; and your own servant shall bear us company. [*to Martin.*] My good master you had better remain here, so that if the familiars should come before we are ready for them, you can be on hand to receive them.

Mar. [*to Eleanor.*] Courage, courage. If there is need of great strength, O, in God's name be strong!

El. You shall see, kind sir. I know that your own safety demands this effort on my part. [*Bardolf and Eleanor exit,* L.]

Mar. The last words which she said sounds in my ears yet.— She would be strong because my safety required it. Such a look! so beautiful, so good, and so pure. I think I shall love her. Folks say that us Christians dare not marry a Jewess. My heart tells me that it is no more wrong to wed a jewess, who is kind, noble and honest than it is to marry a Christian maiden. [*he walks to and fro and puts his hand in his pocket and draws out the paper which Hector gave him.*] God have mercy! I have already slain two men in the keeping of my pledge to the Brotherhood, and in answer to the same I am willing to lay down my life; but I cannot do this fearful thing. O, what a curse would life be to me if my conscience were laden with the recollection of such a deed. The sweet face of the victim would haunt me here and hereafter. [*he replaces the paper in his pocket and takes a seat— he also has his hand reclining on a table. Walter is heard without. Martin listens.*]

Wal. [*without,* R.] Whose dwelling is this?

El. [*without,* R.] It is the abode of Sir Martin Wilsdorf.

Wal. We must see him.

El. I will speak with him, sir, and inform him of your request.

Wal. Don't trouble yourself to do that. Lead the way and we will follow.

Enter WALTER *and three familiars,* D. F., *lead by* ELEANOR, *who is disguised as a common servant.*

El. My master, these gentlemen wish to speak with you.

Wal. Martin Wilsdorf, we have come to search your house; but first, will you let us see the females who are at present beneath your roof?

Mar. I am willing and ready to do any proper thing. But first I should like to know who you are, and whence you come and by what authority you make this demand?

Wal. We come from the holy office, and we are in search of a female who is summoned to appear before that august tribunal.

Mar. Then of course you are at liberty to go where you please. [*to Eleanor.*] Girl, go and call Katrina and Calypso. [*Eleanor exit* R. *and re-enter with Katrina and Calypso,* R.] Here you have the females, gentlemen. There is one more member of my family, however, whom you may chance to find abed.

El. Bardolf is not abed yet, sir. I left him in the kitchen.

Wal. Then in the kitchen we'll find him; so lead the way as directly as you can, for we have much work on our hands. [*Eleanor leads Walter and the familiars off* L. *Martin converses with Katrina and Calypso and sends them off,* R. *Walter is heard without,* L.]

Wal. [*without,* L.] Hallo! Look up here. Are you a woman in disguise?

Bard. [*without,* L.] Eh! What? Holy Mother! who are you? [*the familiars are heard laughing.*]

Wal. We are all gentlemen.

Mar. You can rest assured that you are nothing else but a set of villians! [*aside.*]

Re-enter WALTER *and the three familiars,* L. *followed on with* ELEANOR.

Wal. [*to Martin.*] I think that you are a particular friend of the Margrave.

Mar. I think our prince counts me among the number of his friends.

Wal. You will excuse us for the liberty we have taken, Sir Martin, but we search all dwellings alike, be they the abodes of prince, potentate or priest.

Mar. Every man should do his duty, be it pleasant or not. [*He leads them out,* D. F.—*Eleanor sinks on a chair,* L.—*Martin re-enters.* D. F.] You are weak, lady; this trial has been too much for you.

El. No, no, the ordeal has been a severe one, but I am not weak—not very weak. I shall soon recover from the shock. [*she rises.*]

Mar. I know dear lady, that your task has been hard, but let the reflection that you have passed safely through bear healing to your tried spirit. I believe the worst is over, and if we are careful now, all may be well.

Enter CALYPSO, R.

Here Calypso, take your young mistress to a place of rest. [*Eleanor and Calypso exit* R. *Martin watches them off.*]

Enter BARDOLF EBERSWALD, L.

Bard. Now my master, what think you of my plan?

Mar. It was most excellent. [*taking Bardolf's hand.*] By the mass I owe the maiden's life to you.

Bard. More than that. You may I think truthfully say that we owe the lives of all of us to the happy thought; for upon my soul, I don't believe any other plan could have saved us.

Mar. You are right, my brother.

Bard. And the girl acted her part bravely.

Mar. In truth she did.

Bard. At first she seemed to think she could never sustain herself in the presence of the spies of the inquisition. But when she came to understand that the safety of the man who had thus far served her was at stake, she at once became brave and resolved. What a pity 'tis she's a Jewess.

Mar. Why so, my man?

Bard. Because, what a splendid wife she would make for some Christian gentleman.

Mar. Some such man, for example, as Conrad of Marburg, or Berthold of Baden.

Bard. O, Heaven defend her!

Mar. How, Bardolf.—are they not Christians?

Bard. No! I swear they are not! The Jewess herself is a better Christian than they!

Mar. Then, after all, you admit that the lady possesses some of the Christian graces?

Bard. Yes, certainly. In short, Sir Martin, she lacks only the

SCENE I.]   THE JEWESS OF HEIDELBERG.   53

name. Zounds! she should be converted to the true faith; and if I had your persuasiveness of argument, I think I could convert her. [*Martin smiles.*] Perhaps you think the task would be a hopeless one. Ah, if you know as much as I do—

Mar. And what do you know?

Bard. I know that the beautiful Jewess feels the deepest gratitude towards you. Mercy! how quick the color came to her handsome cheeks, and how her tremulousness stopped, when she thought she had it in her power to save you. I tell you, my master, you must be cautious.

Mar. How?

Bard. You must be cautious.

Mar. Cautious in what?

Bard. In your speech before that girl. I can see—I can see. Ah, she has a very tender heart. If you were a Jew, or if she were a Christian, it might be all right, [*A. knock,* D. F.] Bless me! it is another of the Brotherhood. What can be the matter now.

Mar. Go to the door and ascertain. [*Bardolf opens the door.*]

Enter VICTOR OF ANTIOCH, D. F.

Vic. Good day, Sir Martin. Good day, my brother Bardolf. [*shakes hands with both and takes a seat.*] So you have had a busy day of it.

Mar. Somewhat so. But what have you heard?

Vic. I met Hector close by the bridge, and he told me all he knew. He told me of the death of the Jew; of the death of the two familiars, and of the destruction of Olsheim's house. And he furthermore told me of the search that was being made for the Jew's daughter. Is the damsel here?

Mar. Yes.

Vic. Have the spies been here?

Mar. Yes.

Vic. And found her not?

Mar. No.

Vic. Come, take a seat and explain all. [*Bardolf exit, R. Martin takes a seat near Victor—both converse together, and at the end Victor claps his hands.*] Good! I am glad the girl has been protected, for we owed to her father much gratitude. And since she has thus far escaped the snare of her enemies, we may hope to save her to the end. By the Holy Cross, Wilsdorf, we have much to encourage us. Wherever I travel I find among those who dare to speak, the same enmity to the accursed Inquisition. I tell you, its days are numbered in Germany.

Mar. I hope so.

Vic. You may hope with a strong faith, my brother. Our German people think too much to suffer long under such a fearful burden. Thus far our plans work well, and if we are true to ourselves, there can be no failure. But of this Jewess: I think she is very beautiful.

Mar. She is.

Vic. And I know that the Margrave will do all in his power to gain her. I tell you freely, Wilsdorf, I have taken a strange interest in that girls welfare. [*Martin feels uneasy.*] Be not surprised. I not only have a noble wife living, but I have a daughter almost, if not quite, as old at this Jewess. I sympathize with her because she is in danger from the unholy lust and cupidity of our deadly enemies.

Mar. So do I sympathize with her. And she shall be saved if I have the power to do it.

Vic. And still she is not wholly safe here. In fact, for a while she cannot be considered safe in Heidelberg. You and I both know the character of the Margrave, and we know his power. If we would save the maiden, we must remove her from the city.

Mar. And whither shall she be taken?

Vic. There are many places. In the deep, quiet valleys of the Schwarzwald, among the stout peasants, we can find a safe home. And the sooner we can get her off the better; for, were she to be taken now, the inquisitors might extort from her some things which we might not wish them to know.

Mar. Ah, Victor, you don't know the girl. I am sure she would die before she would betray us.

Vic. Upon my soul, Wilsdorf, you have gained extensive knowledge of the maiden's character.

Mar. Because such characters are very easily read.

Vic. Have a care, or I shall think you regard the beautiful Jewess with some tender emotion. But, be not offended, my brother. Even if you really love her, you must see the soundness of my proposition. The child who has rescued a frightened bird from the jaws of a cat, is apt to concieve a strong friendship for the bird; and so have I conceived a strong friendship for this unfortunate girl. She had better die than fall into the hands of the Margrave.

Mar. Yes, yes.

Vic. Then we must get her away from Heidelberg.

Mar. True. I am acquainted with some of the peasants of the Schwarzwald.

Vic. So am I. But neither you nor I must leave this section at present. I will find means to send her to some safe asylum; and I will furthermore provide her with a suitable companion.

Mar. She already has one companion.

Vic. Do you know the old woman, Calypso?

Mar. Yes.

Vic. I think she had better not go,—at least, not at present. She has long been known as Jacob Olsheim's house-keeper, and she might be recognized. I think I have a better companion for the maiden. However, we will let the matter rest for to-night, and on the morrow we will decide what shall be done. Berthold of Baden shall not gain this prize. [*He goes to* D. F.]

Mar. Not while I live! [*Rising.*]

Vic. Well then on the morrow you can expect me.

[*Exeunt* D. F.]

Mar. [*thinking.*] I know that Victor is a true and honorable man, and I fear not to trust him. And he feels an interest in Eleanor's welfare. And what do I feel? Ah, if it is a sin to love a Jewess, then I fear that I have occasion to look to Heaven for pardon! [*He looks up.*]

[*Picture.—Scene closed in.*]

SCENE II.—*A Plain Chamber.*

Enter BERTHOLD, *the Margrave,* R.

Ber. [*He walks to and fro.*]

Enter CONRAD *of Marburg,* L.

Now Conrad, what is the report?

Con. Nothing favorable.

Ber. [*stamping his foot.*] Donnerwetter! I do not understand it.

Con. Easy, my lord. The girl has not escaped us.

Ber. But there is some deeply laid scheme against us. Do you know, Conrad, what I believe?

Con. No, my lord.

Ber. I believe that there is a secret society growing in Baden, the object of which is to break down the power of the inquisition.

Con. Have you just discovered that?

Ber. Ah,—do you know of the existence of such a society?

Con. I know there is something of the kind, and I will ere long reach the bottom of it. If I can contrive to get one of my trusty familiars into their midst as a member, we shall make short work with the plotters.

Ber. Do it Conrad,—do it as quickly as you can; for I know such a society would hold me in its direst hatred.

Con. Fear not that I shall allow any opportunity to escape me. I have too much at stake. The conspirators shall find themselves at my mercy when they least expect it. Ah, they don't realize what a dangerous thing it is to kick against the holy office.

Ber. Any assistance that I can render to this end you may freely demand of me.

Con. At the proper time, my lord, we shall need your aid— First, however, I must unearth the monster; and that is a work which must be done quietly.

Ber. And now you will turn your attention to this girl. By Heaven! I must have her.

Con. She shall be yours finally. But she must first answer me some questions.

Ber. You do not mean that you will put her to the torture.

Con. We will not harm her.

Ber. By the holy cross, her fair body must not be scarred!— Aye,—more. Your executioners must not lay their hands upon her.

Con. But, my lord, she must be questioned.

Ber. Then let her be questioned at the castle. She will speak quickly under the influence of fear.

Con. I have no objection to that; but we shall not question her until we find her.

Ber. We must find her! If your men have searched the city through, I'll send my soldiers into the country; for she may have fled from Heidelberg.

Con. Now you come to the point. And the sooner you start your troopers off the better.

Ber. I will start them at once. They shall go in small parties and scour every road; and, in the meantime, you will continue to keep watch in the city. [*both exit* L.]

Scene III.—*Martin Wilsdorf's Apartments.*—Sir Martin Wilsdorf—Victor of Antioch *and* Irene *are discovered—they converse together.* Victor *has a small bundle in his hand.*

Mar. But, bless me! You told me her companion should be a female.

Vic. Yes. I had thought of my fair niece, Irene—the daughter of my widowed sister.

Mar. And can she not go?

Vic. Certainly. I have brought her hither for that purpose.

Mar. Where is she?

Vic. O, Wilsdorf, are you so blind that you cannot see? Behold the lady Irene before you!

Mar. [*He is surprised and looks anxiously at Irene.*] Dear lady, then you are going upon this adventure.

Irene. So my uncle says.

Vic. [*to Sir Martin.*] Now, you will call the Jewess.

Mar. Yes. [*exit* R.]

[*Victor and Irene converse together.*]

Re-enter Martin *with* Eleanor, R.

Mar. You will be safer with some of our friends in the Schwarzwald than you can in the city; and we have concluded to send you away as soon as possible.

El. And you will go with me?

Mar. No, lady, that cannot be. My absence from the town might excite suspicion. But I think I can send Bardolf with you.

Vic. Yes. I think your man would be a proper escort.

Mar. And this good friend will also bear you company. [*Eleanor is also surprised at seeing Irene.*]

Irene. [*takes Eleanor's hands.*] I think, lady, that we shall be very good friends.

El. O, you are not a boy!

Vic. [*to Eleanor.*] This is my niece Irene; and I shall be very much disappointed if you do not learn to love her.

El. O, I know I shall love her. [*She kisses Irene.*]

Vic. Lady the sooner preparations are made for your departure the better. Wilsdorf informs me that an old woman who has long been a domestic beneath your roof, is with you; but your own good judgment must tell you that she cannot accompany you. The face of old Calypso is as familiar as was the face of your father; and I greatly wonder that the spies did not detect her last night. She may come to you if you desire, by and by, but she must not go now.

El. Kind sir, I know that you were a friend to my father, and I believe you are a friend to the daughter; so I will trust you.— Point out to me the way of safety from mine enemies, and I will not oppose you.

Vic. I think the way is clear. I have brought with me a suit of clothes like those Irene wears, and you must put them on. [*he gives the bundle to Eleanor.*] After this you two will go to my house, whither we will shortly follow you. Now go with my niece and make the change in your garb. [*Eleanor and Irene exit* R. *arm in arm.*]

Enter BARDOLF EBERSWALD, L.

Bardolf, do you know where the town of Eppingen is?

Bard. I know very well, sir.

Vic. In a deep valley, not more than half a league from Eppingen, to the north-west, lives an old peasant named Andrew Fornbach. If you can find him, and bear a message from me, he will give you shelter.

Bard. I am sure that I can find the place. For I now recollect of having stopped once in that valley when on my way to Ulm. At all events I cannot go amiss. And, if we can get away by noon, and meet with no accident on the way, we can reach the valley to-night, for it is not more than ten leagues distant.

Vic. It is not over nine, and the road is not blind to one who knows its windings.

Mar. You are going away with a very precious charge, and you will not forget that I am deeply interested. I tell you frankly, Bardolf, that I hold the Jewess——

Bard. I know what you mean, and you may rest assured that I will make answer to the trust with my life, if need be. You can give me no caution which I do not already comprehend. [*Martin shakes hands with Bardolf, who afterwards exits* D. F.—*Victor converses with Martin.*]

Re-enter BARDOLF, *ready for travel*, D. F.—*also re-enter* ELEANOR *and* IRENE, R.—*Eleanor is dressed in the garb of a boy as Irene—All except Eleanor and Martin go to the window and converse together.*

El. [*to Martin, taking his hand.*] I am to bid you farewell!

Mar. No, no, dear lady. Let me call you,—Eleanor! my own dear Eleanor! you are not going away with that look—not in that tone. You are not going for a long time; we shall meet again! I bid you adieu! [*He takes from his neck a steel cross and gives it to Eleanor.*] But before you go, take this—it is but a cross; take it for my sake; take it for the sake of the one who placed his life in defence of your own! [*she hesitates to take it.*] Now come, take it. [*he falls on his knees.*] On my knees I beg of you to take this cross. Let me not beg you as I would a child! Take it and remember me. [*she accepts the cross.*]

Vic. [*to Eleanor.*] Make haste, for it is growing late.

Mar. [*taking Eleanor's hand.*] Farewell, Farewell! and God be with you until you can safely return to Heidelberg! [*he shakes*

hands with all except Victor—*Eleanor, Irene, Victor and Bardolf, exeunt*, D. F.—*Martin goes to door and looks after them.*]
I love that girl with all my heart, with all my soul, and with all my might. Eleanor, Eleanor, see here! I wish to speak one word more to you. [*exit*, D. F.]

CURTAIN.—END OF ACT III.

ACT IV.

SCENE I.—*The Woods—Stage quite dark—Thunder and Lightning.*

Enter BARDOLF EBERSWALD, ELEANOR *and* IRENE, L., *in a hurry—Eleanor is dressed as Irene,*

Bard. [*gazing around.*] Beim Heimmel! I fear we shall not reach Eppingen to night,
El. I am not afraid of the rain.
Bard. Ah, you know but little of the power of the storm when it breaks loose in this forest. Mercy! you would'nt live through it. But there is a shelter not far away—perhaps half a league—where we can find rest. [*noise of tramping is heard.* R.]
Irene. Hark!
Bard. I hear it.
El. What is it?
Bard. Somebody is coming.
El. You dont think they are enemies?
Bard. I hope not.
El. If they are, we can hide in the woods. [*all listen.*]
Irene. They are troopers!
El. Are they enemies?

Bard. Let them be what they will, we must put on bold faces. It is too late to avoid them.

El. O, good Bardolf, I see it in your face—they are enemies! They have been sent after us! Are they not servants of the Margrave?

Bard. Yes, lady, and so you have more need of firmness and composure. [*As two soldiers enter* R. *Eleanor tries to escape to* L., *when her hair gets entangled with the branch of a tree close by and her hat is brushed off her head—her hair falls over her shoulders—All gaze at her and are surprised,*]

Irene. [*aside.*] God save us!

1st *Sol.* Ach! Der Teufel und seine Groszmutter! Here is a wondrous head of hair for a boy. As I'm alive, I believe the storm has brought us upon the very prize we seek! [*thunder and lightning.*]

Bard. What is it you want?

1st. *Sol.* We want yonder damsel, for we know that she is the one we seek.

Bard. Both these young people are under my protection, and I shall not let them go without an effort to prevent it. We are peacefully pursuing our way, meaning harm to no one, and I know not by what right or authority you interrupt us.

1st *Sol.* By the holy saints! you'll learn to your cost by what authority we act. If you are acquainted in Heidelberg—and I believe you belong there—you know very well who we are. And now, in the name of the Margrave, we arrest all three of you!

Bard. You'll arrest the three if you arrest one.

1st *Sol.* Zounds! You do not mean to oppose us?

Bard. I shall protect my charge.

1st *Sol.* Ah, fellow, you do not try to deceive us. [*pointing to Eleanor.*] Yonder stands the daughter of Jacob Olsheim, and we will take her back to Heidelberg. And furthermore, we will

SCENE I.] THE JEWESS OF HEIDELBERG. 63

not tarry longer in this storm. [*both soldiers draw their swords.*] Look ye, we would prefer to take ye back alive, but the decision rests not with us; you can die here in the forest if you desire! [*Bardolf also draws.*] Der Teufel! Are you a fool or a madman? Do you wish to die in this pelting storm?

Bard. I would rather die here than give up yonder——[*hesitates.*] Call her a maiden, if you please—call her the daughter of the Jew; but mark you, I will die here before I will give her up! Now come on, and remember that over my dead body you reach your prize. I know whence you come and what dark power you serve! [*Thunder and lightning—Music—Bardolf fights with both soldiers—he kills the first soldier.*]

2d Sol. Surrender! and your life shall be spared.

Bard. We will not waste time in words, for this storm is not at all inviting, and I am in a hurry to be on my way. And when I start, I shall not start towards Heidelberg. Now come on! [*both fight—the soldier gets wounded and still fights on, but his strength fails him—Bardolf stabs him again—the soldier falls and dies—Bardolf sheaths his sword and drags the bodies of the soldiers off,* R.]

El. Alas! How much more blood must be shed on my account!

Bard. [*he picks up Eleanor's hat which has fallen and gives it to her.*] My dear lady, do not allow this to trouble you. Those men have died because they would have consigned you to the hands of a monster. Now gather up those unfortunate tresses and cover your head from the storm. [*she puts on her hat.*] Courage! courage! We'll find shelter by and by. [*all exit,* R.[

Scene II.—*Michael Fostern's Inn*—*a table and four chairs, c*·
—*a door,* F. *and* R. *and* L. *leading to two rooms*—*a fireplace,*
L. *which is seen burning bright*—MICHAEL FORSTERN *is discovered standing by the fire. Thunder and Lightning*

Enter BARDOLF EBERSWALD, ELEANOR *and* IRENE, D. F.

Bard. [*shakes hands with Michael.*] How do you do.

Mich. I'm all right, and how are you?

Bard. The same, thank you. Look here, friend, I wish you would please have a fire made in one of your private rooms, so that these young gentlemen can dry their clothing.

Mich. And who are they?

Bard. They are young students on their way to Ulm, and as they are not overstocked with clothing, it might be more pleasant for them to be alone. Of course for this trouble you shall be well paid, for the parents of the young gentlemen are wealthy.

Mich. I'll call my wife. [*calling,*] Theresa! Theresa! [*Bardolf joins Eleanor.*]

Enter THERESA, R. D.

[*he converses with her.*]

Bard. [*Aside, to Eleanor and Irene.*] While you are drying your clothes, you must keep your door secure; and, above all things, let not a sign of your true sex be given. Guard your voices; keep your hair out of sight; be stout of heart; and betray no fears or trepidation.

El. Shall we have to remain here all night?

Bard. I cannot yet tell. Of one thing, however, you may be assured, I shall leave here as soon as I possibly can. Of course we cannot think of venturing out into this storm again. Mercy! How the wind howls?

Mich. [*to Eleanor and Irene.*] Gentlemen, you will please follow my wife into a warm and comfortable room. [*Theresa leads*

Scene II.]   THE JEWESS OF HEIDELBERG.   65

off Eleanor and Irene, L. D., *thunder and lightning*]   Upon my soul, this is a hard storm.

Bard. [*taking a seat by table*,] Some wine, if you please, [*Michael exit*, R. D., *and re-enter bringing with him a bottle with wine and tumbler—thunder and lightning—Bardolf drinks.*]

Mich. There it is again.

Bard. You are somewhat used to such?

Mich. Yes sir. I have seen many such since I have been in this valley.

Bard. Do you think this one will last long?

Mich. We shall not see the end of it to-day, though I fancy it will spend itself through the night.

Bard. Do you have many travelers this way? [*takes a chair to the fire and sits down.*]

Mich. Not many. Though you are not the first for to-day.

Bard. Yes, yes. I met some travelers a couple of leagues back from here.

Mich. Met them?

Bard. Yes.

Mich. Then they passed not this way.

Bard. Ah—there have been travelers in the other direction!

Mich. Yes,—pursuing the same course with yourself. There were three of them, two of whom were officers.

Bard. Officers?

Mich. I should think they were officers of some kind, At all events, they wore uniforms and were armed.

Bard. And what in the world can armed officers be doing here?

Mich. In search of some escaped criminal, I guess. At all events, they were particular to know if any travelers had passed this way, and they furthermore took it upon themselves to make a thorough search of my premises.

Bard. You said there were only two officers?

Mich. Only two in uniform; but the third man had much to do. In fact, he lead the search, and seemed to have authority. But he was a villianous looking fellow.

Bard. By what authority did they profess to act?

Mich. They said, by authority of the Margrave.

Bard. It would have been a mark of politeness, if nothing more, had they informed you whom they were after.

Mich. Of course it would. Confound their impudence, I should'nt weep if I knew that thunderbolt had fallen upon them and crushed them,—especially the rascal that wore the black robe! They turned my house upside down and never offered to buy a bottle of wine nor a morsel of food. Ah! somebody is coming. [*Michael goes to the* D. F., *he partly opens it and looks out—thunder and lightning.*] Der Teuyfel und seine Groszmutter!

Bard. [*starting up.*] What is it?

Mich. Beim Himmel! Those rascals are coming back! this storm has frightened them.

Bard. [*aside.*] I dare not trust this man. But what shall I do. It would not do to take the girls out into this storm. Ha! I have it—[*draws Michael away from the door.*] Michael, is not your boy at hand?

Mich. Yes.

Bard. Then let him attend to those people, and do you come with me, I have something of the utmost importance to say.

Mich. Whither will you go?

Bard. Anywher so that we can speak in private. I pray you grant me the favor. Let the boy attend to the troopers.

Mich. [*thinking.*] Well. You may follow me into that room. [*pointing to* R. D.—*both exit there.*]

SCENE III.—*A Plain Room in Michael Forstern's Inn.*
Enter BARDOLF *and* MICHAEL, R.

THE JEWESS OF HEIDELBERG.

Bard. Michael Forstern, do you know who those people are that have just stopped before your gate?

Mich. They are people whom I have no occasion to fear.

Bard. One of them is a spy of the inquisition.

Mich. And why should I fear a messenger from that holy institution. [*he makes the sign of a cross upon his bosom*]

Bard. [*he starts at seeing the sign, and also makes the same sign.*] I don't know why either of us should fear!

Mich. [*gazing into Bardolf's face sharply.*] Eh! You are from Antioch?

Bard. From Tyre.

Mich Your name?

Bard. Henry.

Mich. Is it true?

Bard. Satisfy yourself,

Mich. The Son of God bore a Cross.

Bard. So do I.

Mich. That cross was of wood.

Bard. Mine is of steel.

Mich. So is mine; and we are Brothers well met. [*both shake hands together.*]

Bard. Aye, we are most exceedingly well met; [*taking from his neck the cross which Sir Joseph Verdin gave him and holds it to view.*] And by this sign, I demand your assistance.

Mich. If you need it in our just cause, my life is yours. I can only beg that you will be circumspect and discreet. [*Bardolf puts the cross around his neck again.*]

Bard. My Brother, you shall know how much 'need I have; and since I find you to be one of our sacred order, I will trust you fully. My traveling companions are not boys.

Mich. Eh!

Bard. Not boys, Michael, but both girls. Do you know Victor of Antioch?

Mich. Our deputy grand Master?

Bard. The same.

Mich. Certainly I know him.

Bard. He it was who sent me upon my present mission. One of the girls is his niece, and the other is the daughter of Jacob Olsheim, the Jew. This fair young Jewess is the very person these villians are in search of. And not only has Conrad of Marburg set his hounds upon her track, but the Margrave of Baden has joined in the unholy work. Her father has already been sacrificed and now they would lay their bloody hands upon the daughter.

Mich. Do you mean that Jacob Olsheim has been killed?

Bard. Yes.

Mich. God have mercy on us! [*crossing himself.*] When shall this work stop?

Bard. I hope before long. And now we must turn our attention to saving these girls. How shall it be done?

Mich. Will not their boy's garbs protect them?

Bard. I fear not. The troopers might be misled, but that rascally spy is not so easily to be deceived. I tell you plainly, my brother, if the worst comes, the lives of those three men must not stand in my way.

Mich. I would avoid bloodshed, if possible. Can you not think of some plan? I will assist you.

Bard. What know these men of your family matters?

Mich. Nothing at all.

Bard. Is your wife to be trusted?

Mich. Yes.

Bard. And your boy?

Mich. Yes.

SCENE III.]   THE JEWESS OF HEIDELBERG.   69

Bard. Then the girls must don new disguises and must pass for members of your family. You can say that they have come in from the forest since the storm broke. Bring your wife to me at once and then you may go and attend to your guests.

[*Michael exit* R. *and re enter* R. *with Theresa.*]

Mich. Theresa will help us,

Theresa. That I will. Michael has told me that your companions are girls, and that they are in mortal danger. I will help you if I can.

Bard. You can help us very essentially. We must put new disguises upon them. What have you?

Theresa. We can make a girl and a boy of them. A suit of Francis' clothes will answer for one of them, and we can easily manage a dress for the other.

Bard. Let it be so. And now Michael, go you and attend to your guests. If they ask touching new arrivals, tell them that one has come—one only. If they have discovered the three horses and ask whose they are, just say they belong to the single traveler, and if they would know more, bid them wait until I come.

[*Michael exit* R. *and Bardolf and Theresa exit* L.]

SCENE IV.—*Michael Forstern's Inn.*

WALTER *and two soldiers are discovered sitting by the fire. Thunder and Lightning.*

Enter BARDOLF EBERSWALD, R. D.

Bard. [*seating himself by the fire.*] A good day to you, gentlemen.

1*st Sol.* } The same to you sir.
2*d Sol.*

[*Walter eyes Bardolf sharply.*]

Bard. This is a great storm, gentlemen. But I hope it will be over by to-morrow morning, as I have quite a way to travel.— But may I ask you where you are from?

Wal. We are from Heidelberg, and are on our way to Mainhardt. And now may I ask where you are from?

Bard. Certainly, sir. I am from Mannheim, and I am on my way to Ulm.

Wal. On business.

Bard. Partly on business, and partly on pleasure. I am not blessed with many friends, nor am I burdened with much business; but friends and business together offer inducement enough to lead me upon the journey.

Wal. Do you bring any news from Mannheim?

Bard. Nothing of importance.

Wal. When did you leave there?

Bard. Three days ago.

Wal. Do you travel alone?

Bard. In one sense, yes; and in another, no. I have some four legged companions.

Wal. Eh!

Bard. I am taking some extra horses along with me.

Wal. Do you expect to find use for them on the road?

Bard. No. I am taking them for a friend. They are simply entrusted to my care for safe delivery in Ulm.

Wal. Might I ask your name?

Bard. Certainly. My name is Eberswald. And in return, may I ask what your name is?

Wal. I am called Walter.

Enter MICHAEL FORSTERN *and* THERESA, R. D.—*they bring a table with them—supper is on the table.*

Mich. Gentlemen, supper is ready. [*exit* D. F. *All except Theresa seat themselves around the table and eat.*]

Theresa. [*calling.*] Joseph! Joseph!

Enter ELEANOR *disguised as a peasant, her face is rather soiled,* R, D.

[*Theresa converses with Eleanor and sends her off* L. D.—*Walter watches Eleanor closely. Theresa calls again.*] Francena! Bring in the hot muffins.

Enter IRENE *disguised as a common servant. She brings in the muffins on a plate and puts it on the table, and exit* R. D.

Wal. Are these your children, my good woman?

Theresa. No, sir. We have no children of our own. The boy and girl are children of my husband's only sister.

Wal. Where does your husband's sister live?

Theresa. She is at present residing in Strasburg.

Wal. She is the mother of two promising children. Has she others?

Theresa. No, sir.

Wal. I should think she would like their companionship and assistance of at least one of her children.

Theresa. Ah, kind sir, she is herself but a servant.

Wal. That will do. [*Theresa exit* R. D.]

1st Sol. [*to Walter.*] Of course we cannot leave this place to-night.

Wal. No. [*all rise from the table.*]

1st Sol. Then I think we'll look to our horses, and after that find our beds; for, if the storm ceases, we may wish to be off early.

Wal. A very good thought. [*to Bardolf.*] What think you my friend, will this storm break up to-night?

Bard. Indeed, sir, I cannot tell. I am not qualified to judge weather-signs in this forest. Our host might give you the information. [*He goes to* R. D., *partly opens it and stands without listening.*]

Wal. [*He looks around.*] I have something to say—Sh!—But not here. Let us go to the stable.

1st Sol. }
2d Sol. } What is it?

[*Bardolf steals himself from* R. D. *and exits* D. F.]

Wal. Obey me and come. [*All exeunt softly,* D. F.]

Scene V.—*A Wood.*

Enter Bardolf, L.

Bard. So, so, my fine man, you have something to say, have you! I'll listen to every word—Ha! here they come? [*he hides himself,* R.]

Enter Walter *and the two Soldiers,* L.

1st Sol. Now what is it?

Wal. ——Sh! Let not your words be too loud; I think we have hit upon something of importance.

1st Sol. Eh,—how so?

Wal. Did you particularly notice that fellow who pretends to have come from Mannheim?

1st Sol. }
2d Sol. } Yes.

Wal. And did it strike you that you had ever seen him before? [*both soldiers shake their heads—No—*] I know that I have seen him, and I know that he belongs in Heidelberg.

1st Sol. Ha! then he is deceiving us.

Wal. Of course he is, and I can tell you one thing more:—I have seen one of those horses within a week in our city. The rascal is imposing upon us. If he has deceived us in one thing, he has probably deceived us in others. Those three horses belong in Heidelberg.

1st. Sol. What more?

Wal. [*all go and stand by the* 2 E. R., *looking in.*] Much more. The horses are fully caparisoned, and I am sure that they have all been ridden to-day. [*stepping within* R. 2 E.] Do you observe that these reins have all been held tightly in the hand since the storm came. Just notice here: [*the soldiers also go in-*

SCENE V.] THE JEWESS OF HEIDELBERG. 73

side] See where the hands grasped this rein. You not only see that it is gathered up here, but in this spot it is not so wet. Look at the saddles too, why are they all three so dry? [*All re-enter,* R. 2 E.[

1*st Sol.* } Der Teuyfel!
2*d Sol.*

Wal. That means something.

1*st Sol.* Certainly. It means that the man did not come here alone. But who came with him?—thats the question!

Wal. I think that the son and daughter of our hosts only sister came with him.

1*st Sol.* Eh! What mean you?

Wal. I mean that there must be sleepless eyes in this house to night. A woman can lie as well as a man. I know that this stranger has lied to us, for I know that he came from Heidelberg, and that two companions came with him. This knowledge led me to watch that boy and girl who were not here when we called in the morning, and if the seeming boy is not a fair-faced damsel then I am mistaken.

1*st Sol.* Holy saints! do you think she is the one we seek?

Wal. Of that I am determined to satisfy myself; and to this end a strict watch must be kept through the night. We will go to our chamber and there arrange our plans. I will watch first, and when I am sleep I will call for a relief. Be very careful and let nothing betray the knowledge you have gained.

1*st Sol.* But this old publican.

Wal. He is an imposter and a protector of heretics! If we find the Jewess beneath his roof, he will be food for flames very shortly. [*Walter and both soldiers exit* L.]

Bard. [*creeps from his hiding place and whistles low.*] That infernal rascal suspects us. He is smarter than I had thought. [*mockingly.*] Be very careful and let nothing betray the knowledge you have gained. But O, Mr. Walter, as you call yourself;

You did not think that I was and am now watching you. By the Holy Cross that is in my bosom, I swear that the Jewess shall not fall into the hands of these men—if they do take her, it will be over my dead body! I must hurry to the inn, for the villians may inquire for me. [*exit* L.]

SCENE VI.—*Michael Forstern's Inn.*
WALTAR *and the two Soldiers are discovered sitting around the table drinking*—MICHAEL *is also discovered standing near them.*

Wal. Your health, old man. [*drinks.*] But where is our good friend?

Mich. Here he comes.

Enter BARDOLF EBERSWALD, D. F.

Bard. Am I wanted? [WALTER *and the Soldiers eye Bardolf very closely.*]

Wal. I was wondering if you had gone to bed.

Bard. Not quite yet. I have satisfied myself, however, that I shall have a comfortable place to sleep in. Zounds! how the rain beats down upon the roof. [*to Michael.*] Have you got a lantern handy?

Mich. I think my boy has left one in the stable.

Bard. All right. I will look at my horses, and then I think I will go to bed too. [*exit* D. F.]

Wal. Show us our chamber, old man, for we wish to go to bed.

Mich. [*goes and pushes open the* R. D.] This way, gentlemen. [*Walter and the two soldiers exeunt* R. D. *Michael keeps looking in.*] turn to your right. and you will find a door, open it, and you will find a room—look around and you will find three beds. Ah! there they go right in. [*he shuts the door.*]

Enter BARDOLF, D F.

Bard. [*in a whisper.*] Have they gone to bed?

Mich. Yes.

Bard. Michael, there is trouble ahead.

Mich. I know there is, or at any rate, I have reason to believe there is. I know these rascals suspect you.

Bard. Ah, my brother, they suspect more than that; they suspect you, too.

Mich. Ha!

Bard. ———Sh! That black-robed rascal has ears at every point. I was in the stable while they were there. I was hidden behind some straw, and I heard the whole. Listen! The spy told the troopers that he has seen me in Heidelberg, and that the Jewess is here. And he also said I was an imposter, and if they find the Jewess beneath your roof you will be food for the flames very shortly.

Mich. Mercy! Then I am in for it!

Bard. I am sorry, my brother, but so it seems to be, and the question is:—How shall we all escape?

Mich. By the holy saints! we must kill the rascals!

Bard. That may not be so easily done, for they will not all sleep. I wish we had more help.

Mich. [*goes to the* D. F., *looks out and returns.*] The storm will not break before midnight. By heavens! there is one source of hope. If I could but get a horse out!

Bard. That is impossible, Michael. The spy takes the first watch, and I know that a horse could not be moved from the stable without attracting his attention. But what would you do?

Mich. I would go to Sinsheim.

Bard And what would you do there!

Mich. We have true and faithful Brothers there.

Bard Brothers of the Steel Cross?

Mich. Yes.

Bard. How far is it?

Mich. Two leagues.

Bard. Why bless your soul, you can walk there in two hours: Is not the path plain?

Mich. Yes—to one who knows it.

Bard. And you know it?

Mich. Perfectly.

Bard. Then away you go. It is now not more than nine o'clock—three hours yet to midnight. You have plenty of time. Bring with you the help and we'll take the rascals prisoners. Do you not know of some place where they can be locked up?

Mich. We can find such a place; though, by my faith, I'd rather see their throats cut. I shall never be safe again while they live.

Bard. I don't wish to shed more blood, if I can help it. But still you must not suffer. However, we'll capture them first, and then determine what further to do. And now what say you?

Mich. I am off.

Enter THERESA, R. D.

Theresa. What is the matter, Michael?

Mich. Matter enough! They suspect us, and I must immediately go to Sinsheim for help. By heaven we must take those rascals prisoners. Now, my wife, what say you?

Theresa. You can do just as you think best, but you must be quick about it, too.

Mich. Bring my hat and I will go right away. [*Theresa exit—Bardolf and Michael converse together—re-enter Theresa, bringing Michael's hat—she gives it to him—he puts it on.*]

Bard. Remember, Michael, time is precious. If we are watchful and true, it shall not be long before these beasts of the abominble inquisition will have occasion to flee before us. [*Michael shakes hands with both and exit,* D. F.—*thunder and lightning.*]

Theresa. I will not tell the girls of this; they have both gone to bed and they had better rest in peace.

Bard. You are right Theresa. They need rest and they shall have it. I will lay down here and sleep a little. I think I shall awake when your husband returns. Be under no apprehension of serious danger, for the rascals shall die before they bring harm to you. [*exit Theresa,* R. D., *Bardolf sits on a chair by the table—he falls asleep—stage dark—Music—enter* WALTER *and the two soldiers,* R. D., *softly—Walter has a candle in his hand—they approach Bardolf who is still sleeping on.*]

Wal. ——Sh! He sleeps! Make no noise! [*He takes Bardolf's sword and the soldiers bind him to the chair on which he sits—Walter holds the candle in front of Bardolf's face, who awakes, is surprised, and tries to free himself, but cannot.*]

Bard. Holy Saint Peter! What does this mean?

Wal. Can you not imagine?

Bard. No sir. I can imagine nothing.

Wal. Then your imagination must be very dull. To tell you the truth, my dear sir, we fear that you have strayed away from your home. We think your senses are somewhat shattered. Do you really imagine that you belong in Mannheim?

Bard. No sir, I don't belong in Mannheim. I simply told you that I was on my way from Mannheim. I belong in Saxony.

Wal. Never mind. We'll arrive at the truth without further assistance from you. The most that we shall require at your hands will be quiet submission; and to this end I think we had better render you a little further help. [*He gives the light to one of the soldiers, and takes from his pocket a handkerchief and binds Bardolf's mouth—Bardolf again tries to free himself, but cannot. They leave Bardolf, and exeunt* L. D.—*they leave the door partly open—Irene is heard without* L. D.]

Irene. [*without* L. D.] Mercy! Who is that?

SCENE VI.] THE JEWESS OF HEIDELBERG. 78

Wal. Easy, my pretty lass. Der Teuyfel! What is this by your side? [*Eleanor is heard uttering a sharp cry.*] Look ye, my fair damsels, I hav'ent time to ask questions now. You will get up and dress yourselves as quickly as possible. Come—you will save yourselves much trouble by obeying me.

Irene. But, sir, you will not force us to arise in your unseemly presence.

Wal. My two companions shall turn their backs while you dress. I can accommodate you so far, but no farther.

El. [*without* L. D.] We are lost! lost! lost!

Irene. Hush! Even though death comes, let us meet it bravely. We cannot resist—so let us obey.

Wal. Shall we lift you to the floor?

Irene. No, sir. We will arise. But, sir, will you not tell us what you mean? Why are you here? What have we done?

Wal. I will answer you your questions when you have arisen. [*a pause.*] Ah! You were not the one who wore the boys garb.

Irene. When it pleases our fancy, sir, we both wear boys clothes.

Wal. Upon my soul, you have curious tastes.

Irene. We simply have taste for comfort, sir. These garbs are better suited for traveling in the forest than are the frocks and robes of the female. Come, sister.

Wal. You make a most comely boy. What a pity you must give up so befitting a garb.

1st Sol. Egad! If we hav'ent found our prize, then I'm mistaken.

Wal. Come, my men, make haste and take these ladies.

Irene. Hold, sirs! If you will lead the way, we will follow.

Wal. Then follow me. And you may be left to move of your own accord if you move quickly.

Re-enter WALTER *and the two soldiers,* L. D. *followed in by* ELEANOR *and* IRENE —*they are dressed in the garb of boys*—*the same dress as in Act* 1V. *Scene* I. [*Eleanor and Irene do not see Bardolf.*]

El. O! Where is Bardolf?

Wal. [*pointing to Bardolf.*] Behold him there!

El.
Irene. } [*both shrink away and weep.*] All is lost! lost!—

[*Walter and the soldiers retire,* R.]

El. O, better for me had I died with my father. I should not have dragged others into the pit with me!

Irene. Hush! We may find friends in Heidelberg. Think not of me. God will not forsake us. But see! Bardolf is also taken. I will try and set him free. [*she is about going to Bardolf, but Walter sees her, and he pushes her away—she shrinks away weeping—the soldiers open the door,* F.—*the noise of tramping of horses is heard—all listen.*]

1*st Sol.* I think somebody is coming!

Wal. And who is coming?

1*st Sol.* [*still looking out,* D. F.] Our host, and a band of armed men!

Irene. [*aside—falling on her knees.*] Thank Heaven! We shall be saved.

Wal. [*rushing to* D. F. *and looks out.*] O, yes it is he.— Look to your weapons, my men, and be prepared. It may be that they are enemies. But the rascals cannot know with whom they have to deal.

1*st Sol.* We had better make our escape, if we can. It may be a stronger party than we are. [*Walter and the soldiers rush to the* C. *and stand with their swords drawn.*]

Enter MICHAEL FORSTERN *and three men,* D. F.—*they are all armed with swords.*

SCENE VI.]   THE JEWESS OF HEIDELBERG.   80

Mich. Hallo! You're a precious set of villians, ar'nt ye?
Wal. Why have you brought these companions with you?
Mich. To help me do my work. [*Sees Bardolf and Eleanor and Irene.*] Ah—there they are. And I believe Bardolf is bound too. [*he approaches Bardolf, but is stopped by Walter.*] We want yonder damsels and we want that man!
Wal. You can't have them!—Look ye, you know not upon what dangerous ground you are venturing. What I do, I do by authority of the highest tribunal in the land.
Mich. Eh,—are you from the Emperor?
Wal. No. I am an officer of the Holy Inquisition!
Mich. We don't recognize any such authority, so you'll give us up those prisoners without delay.
Wal. Fool! You are rushing upon your own death! Do you know what it is to resist the authority of the inquisition?
Mich. I know what it is to arrest a set of villians! So we'll not only take your prisoners from you, but we'll take you too.
Wal. Holy angels! these men are mad! To my side, soldiers and strike to the earth the first that dares approach! [*the soldiers stand by Walter with their swords drawn—Michael and his men also draw their swords and stand ready to fight.*] Cut them down!
Mich. Its war to the death! You have given the battle cry, and you must abide the issue! [*Michael's men fight with Walter and the two soldiers—Michael rushes to the side of Bardolf and sets him free—Eleanor and Irene at seeing Michael rush to his side, and shake hands with him in enjoyment—The two soldiers fall and die—Walter at seeing that his soldiers fall tries to escape through* D. F. *but is stopped by a man running to the* D. F. *who has his sword drawn across it—Bardolf also sees it.*]
Bard. In Heaven's name, let not that bloody rascal escape! [*He rushes from his seat and takes a sword from a man close*

by and stands facing *Walter.*.] Stand back, villian! and fight with me, hand to hand. I am from Heidelberg! and yonder stands the daughter of Jacob Olsheim! the person you seek. I have but little time, so come on and fight! [*Bardolf and Walter fight together*—*Walter falls and dies*—*Characters looking on. Elea- and Irene fall on their knees in a prayer. All shout Hurrah for the Brotherhood of the Steel Cross! Picture, &c.*]

CURTAIN.—END OF ACT IV.

ACT V.

SCENE I.—*The Forest*—THERWALD *is discoversd sitting on a rock,* L,—*he is disguised as a Pilgrim.*
Enter BARDOLF EDERSWALD, ELEANOR *and* IRENE, L.

Ther. [*as they enter Therwald arises and stands himself before them.*] A God's blessing upon thee, noble sir!

Bard. Do you want alms?

Ther. [*he looks at Eleanor and Irene very sharply.*] I am weary and hungry; I have walked far and have fared poorly.

Bard. I have no food, but I can give you that which will purchase it. [*He gives Therwald some money.*]

Ther. Thank thee, kind sir.

Bard. You have not been out in the storm?

Ther. I found protection in a deep cave not far from here, where I kept dry, but where I came near starving. Can you not tell me where I may find an inn?

Bard. Yes. There is one a league and a half behind us.

Ther. Ah, good sir, I wish not to go in that direction.

Bard. Then push on towards Eppingen.

SCENE I.]   THE JEWESS OF HEIDELBERG.   82

Ther. How far is it?
Bard. Not more than two or three leagues.
Ther. Are you bound thither?
Bard. I am bound to Ulm, and I am in haste too. The road to Eppingen is plain and direct, and you cannot miss it. [*all exeunt except Therwald,* R., *who watches them off and takes off his disguise.*]
Ther. Ha! ha! ha! You did not think with whom you were speaking. [*he looks at the pilgrim dress.*] Just with this simple dress I'm a pilgrim, and with the dress I have on I am a familiar and an officer of the holy Inquisition!—But those two young men, who can they be? [*thinking.*] Why those same faces I have seen in Heidelberg some three days ago.—Der Teuyfel! one of them must be the daughter of Jacob Olsheim, the one we seek! If that is not a damsel in men's clothes, then I'm mistaken. Now for my horse, and then to follow them. [*exit* L.]

SCENE II.—*Andrew Farnbach's Inn—Bar* 3 L. E.—*A table,* R. *wine and two glasses is on the table—Andrew Fornbach is discovered standing behind the bar.*

Enter BARDOLF, ELEANOR *and* IRENE, L. 1 E.

Bard. I seek Andrew Fornbach. [*Eleanor and Irene take seats and converse together.*]
Andrew. For what?
Bard. I bear a message from a Knight of Antioch.
Andrew. Ha!—from Victor?
Bard. Yes.
Andrew. Then you are from Antioch?
Bard. From Tyre.
Andrew. Your name?
Bard. Henry.
Andrew. Is it true?

Bard. Satisfy yourself.

Andrew. [*taking Bardolf's hand.*] I need ask no more, for I know we are brothers.

Bard. Aye, and well met. [*both converse together, and at the end Andrew expresses astonishment!*]

Andrew. What sayest thou?

Bard. Those two persons who are sitting there are ladies! That one [*points to Eleanor,*] is the daughter of Jacob Olsheim. The Jew. Her father, poor man, is already dead. The familiars arrested him one evening and murdered him. Now Berthold, the black-hearted Berthold—and Conrad, wish to arrest his daughter,

Andrew. [*calling.*] Margaret, Margaret!

Enter MARGARET, 3 R. E.

[*Andrew converses with her and approaches Eleanor and Irene*] You will be safe here, at least for a season, so put away your fears, and make yourself as comfortable as possible.

El. Thank you. [*to Bardolf.*] You will not leave us, good Bardolf.

Bard. Not yet lady; when I am ready to depart you shall have notice. [*Margaret joins Eleanor and Irene.*]

Mar. Poor girls, you must be very tired. Come with me and get some refreshments.

El. Thank you, kind friend, we shall do so. [*exit Margaret followed off by Eleanor and Irene,* R. 3 E.]

Bard. [*aside.*] Ah, she confides in me because I am serving Sir Martin! If I am not most wondrously mistaken, while I have charge of her I have charge of my master's heart! [*to Andrew.*] You are a sworn member of our fraternity?

Andrew. Certainly. The wife of Victor of Antioch is a cousin of mine, so that noble knight knew me and trusted me. If none of our enemies have tracked you hither, I feel sure that the Jewess will be perfectly safe beneath my roof. But, should there be danger, I have hiding places close at hand, known only to my wife and myself. If you wish to return to Heidelberg, you can do so without fear of the result so far as matters here are concerned.

Bard. I feel that I ought to return at once. Victor and my, master must know what adventures I have had upon the road.

Andrew. They should know certainly. The only question is can there be danger to yourself in returning so soon?

Bard. No. For saving Michael Forstern and his wife, those with whom I have spoken upon the road, are past all power of troubling me. There is one man, however—a poor pilgrim—who hailed me; but he is probably in Eppingen ere this. I will go and tell the girls about this—Ah, here they come.

Enter ELEANOR *and* IRENE, R. 3 E.

I think Sir Martin will be very anxious to hear from you, and I have made up my mind to see him very shortly.

Irene. Aye, and my uncle will be very anxious too. I think you had better go, good Bardolf. [*Andrew exit* L. 1 E.]

Bard. If I go, I shall go at once, ladies, and I can only admonish you to be very careful and circumspect. I do not apprehend any immediate danger, but still there is no telling what may happen.

Irene. If danger comes, sir, it shall not come through any want of caution on our part. Our hostess is a true friend I am sure, and I think her husband will not fail us.

Bard. I can promise for Fornbach.

El. How long must this continue? How long must my friends be in danger on my account? How long shall I be hunted like an outcast and a felon?

Bard. I hope not long dear lady, but you will not worry on account of your friends. What we do we do cheerfully; and while we serve you we are at the same time serving the cause of humanity throughout the empire. Bear up a little while and the end may be bright.

Irene. [*to Eleanor.*] It may be brighter than you think.

ANDREW FORNBACH appears L. 1 C. and stands there.

Andrew. My Brother, everything is ready for your departure.

Bard. [*to Eleanor, taking her hand.*] I will tell my master that I left you safe and well, sweet lady.

El. Yes.

Bard. And is there any word you would send?

El. [*tears start in her eyes.*] Tell him that God will bless him for all his kindness to the poor Jewess!

Bard. I will tell him. [*he shakes hands with Eleanor and Irene and exit with Andrew Fornbach* L. 1 E.—*Eleanor and Irene seat themselves.*]

El. Alas! What a sad lot is mine!

Irene. And yet, sweet sister, the sadness of to-day may be changed to joy on the morrow.

El. [*shaking her head.*] No, no, there can be no more joy to me on earth. All that I loved have gone!

Irene. Eleanor, I ought to chide you for that speech.

El. Forgive me, I know that you love me.

Irene. And am I the only one? [*a pause.*] Am I the only living thing you love?

El. You do not understand me, Irene. I meant not that my heart was cold. I love those who love me.

Irene. Then you love good Bardolf?

El. Yes.

Irene. And you ought to love my uncle Victor.

El. I do love him.

Irene. And you should love old Michael Forstern.

El. How can I help loving him.

Irene. And our present kind host.

El. I love him, too.

Irene. And there is one other who has served you—a brave and noble knight. Surely you should not forget in your love, Martin Wilsdorf. [*Eleanor looks pale and drops her head upon her bosom—Irene is surprised.*] Have you no love for Martin Wilsdorf?

El. O God! How can I love him!

Irene. Mercy! Why should you love the others who have been kind to you, and not love him!

El. Don't! Don't! You know not what you say.

Irene. I know very well what I say. I know that of all who have befriended you, not one is more worthy of your deepest gratitude than is Wilsdorf.

El. O, Irene, I am grateful. God knows I feel the deepest gratitude.

Irene. And yet you feel not towards him as you feel towards the others.

El. [*gazes into Irene's face.*] You are cruel, my sister.

Irene. Hush, my dear Eleanor, you know I cannot be cruel to you. Not many possess what you possess.

El. How mean you?

Irene. A heart so true and noble. A love so single and devoted.

El. Irene!

Irene. Ah, Eleanor, that warm heart of yours is not a fit place for secrets. If Martin Wilsdorf could know what I know.

El. He would know how grateful I am.

Irene. Aye! And he would know how deeply you loved him. Hush, my sister, you know I speak the truth.

El. And yet it is not all true.

Irene. What part is untrue?

El. The Christian Knight cannot love the daughter of a Jew.

Irene. Heart to heart! Soul to soul! What has love to do with such empty words. As true as I live the noble Knight loves you.

El. And yet he would not dare to take the Jewess for a wife!

Irene. I can tell you what he would not dare to do. He would not dare to do a wicked thing. If he loves you, his love is pure and holy, and you are held to his heart as a sacred treasure. [*Eleanor weeps.*] My precious one, I have not meant to move you thus. I have only aimed to give you hope and joy for the future. Before I saw you I knew that Wilsdorf loved you; and since I have been with you, I have become assured that you love him.— Look up, Eleanor. Am I not right?

El. I never loved before as I have learned to love now. If to feel that in all the world there is but one tie that binds me to the earth; if to feel that in all the world there is but one shrine at which I can lay my heart; if to feel that life would be a burden were that heart-offering coldly refused, then I love Martin Wilsdorf.

Irene. Now Eleanor, we are friends indeed. I know what it is to love. I will not take your secret without giving you my own. I too love a valiant Knight—a companion-in-arms of Martin Wilsdorf. You have heard of Baldwin?

El. Yes.

Irene. I am his affianced. We shall be married when there is peace in Baden.

El. Alas! I am not so happy. In all the future I see no such joy for me!

Irene. You know not what the future may bring forth, my sister.

El. Ah, the future cannot make me less the child of an outcast race!

Irene. O, how wildly you talk. If Wilsdorf seeks those graces which alone can adorn the christian character, he will find them all in you. As I live, I believe he has no thought else than your beauty and your goodness. When he knows that you love him be sure he will ask no more. I know it would please him if you could assume the christian name; but I also know that he would rather take to himself the pure heart of the Jewess, than bask in the smiles of the christian maiden who possessed not the virtues that make the life as beautiful as the person. Ah! somebody comes.

Enter ANDREW FORNBACH, L. 1 E.

Andrew. [*approaches them.*] Don't be alarmed. I only want you to see a visitor of mine.

Irene. Is it any one whom we know?

Andrew. That is for you to determine. You shall see him, but I do not mean that he shall see you. It is a man in the garb of a pilgrim, and I suspect that it is the same that you met beyond Eppingen. If you will follow me, I will show him to you.

Irene. I will go. [*to Ealenor.*] You may remain here. If it is the same man I shall know him. [*Eleanor keeps her seat—Irene and Andrew go to* L. 1 E. *and stand there looking without—they speak softly.*]

Andrew. Look straight down there, and you will see him.—Who is it?

Irene. It is the man we met upon the road. [*both rejoin Eleanor.*]

Andrew. You are sure that is the man?

Irene. Yes, sir. I cannot be mistaken.

Andrew. Then I fear that he is nothing more nor less than a spy. You need not be alarmed, though I am free to tell you that there may be need of great caution.

El. Do you think the man suspects that we are here?

88   THE JEWESS OF HEIDELBERG.   [ACT V.

Andrew. Yes. I think he more than suspects. I think he followed you from beyond Eppingen, and saw you take shelter here.

Irene. But, can it be possible that he suspects who we are?

Andrew. Of that I am not satisfied. I am going to see him again; and now that I have this clue, I can easily find out if he is to be dreaded. Remain where you are until I come back, and do not give yourselves any unnecessary alarm. [*exit* L. 1 E.]

Irene. Wait, Eleanor. There may be no danger after all.

El. O, I cannot give up my life now! If—— Alas, I am very foolish.

Irene. No, no, my sister—you are not foolish. If what?

El. If he loves me.

Irene. Hush! Your hope is not a vain one.

El. But there is something terrible, Irene, in this gloom and doubt. O, I wish Bardolf were with us. There is danger—I know there is.

Irene. Then let us trust our kind host. He will help us if help be needed.

Re-enter ANDREW FORNBACH, L. 1 E.

Andrew. The man has gone. And it is not impossible that he may come back. At all events, I think you had better not remain in the cot over night. Not far from here there is a mountain cave where you can find shelter and safety, and as soon as possible, I will lead you thither. I have questioned the stranger all I dared, and I know that his coming was for some purpose. I cannot tell you all that I said, nor all that he said; but I can assure you he knows that the three travelers whom he met on the road stopped here; and I fear that he suspects more. He knows that the man who accompanied you has returned; and when I caught the significant glances of his restless eyes, I knew that he thought more than he spoke.

Irene. Did he profess to have any errand here?

Andrew. No. He said he had intended to go to Eppingen, but that he had lost his way.

Irene. That is false. For Bardolf pointed out the direct road to him.

Andrew. Of course it was false. For no man would have thought of leaving the high road and turning into a narrow path on such an errand. However, we have fair warning, and we can be prepared. The sooner we go the better, for I am sure that you would have unwelcome visitors did you remain here. My wife, of her own accord, followed the seeming pilgrim to the narrow pass towards Eppingen, where she saw him lead a horse from the thicket, which he mounted as nimbly as an experienced trooper.

El. I think we had better go from this cot right away.

Andrew. All right. Now come. And we'll show the rascals that we have given them the slip this time. [*all exeunt* L. 1 E.]

SCENE III.—*The woods—Stage quite dark.*

Enter ELEANOR, IRENE *and* ANDREW, L.—*they go across the stage*, R. *and are about to exit, but when* THERWALD *and three soldiers appear* R. *they recoil and try to escape* L., *but the soldiers run after them and catch them. Therwald tears Eleanor's hat off her head and holds her.*

Ther. Aha, my pretty bird, we've caught you, eh! Bless my soul, how kind you were to come to us so readily. Did you know we were here waiting for you?

A Sol. Which is the Jewess?

Ther. [*pointing to Eleanor.*] This. I have seen the face before in her father's house. Ho! ho! Our work thrives. Look to the old man, some of you; for our master Conrad may have use for him. [*The soldiers seize Andrew and carry him off* R. *One soldier takes Irene, and Therwald is about to seize Eleanor by the hands, when she tears herself from him and stands still.*]

El. Lead the way, and I will follow! [*Exit Therwald* R. *followed off by Eleanor weeping.*]

SCENE IV.—*Martin Wilsdorf's Apartments. Sir Martin Wilsdorf and Victor of Antioch are discovered. As scene opens Bardolf Eberswald appears* D. F.—*He shakes hands with both.*

Mar. Ha, my good Bardolf, I can see by your face that you have been successful.

Bard. The girls are safe, sir.

Mar. Thank God!

Vic. I thought there could be no trouble.

Bard. Ah, but there was trouble enough, as you shall quickly hear. [*takes a seat.*] When we arrived in the forest, we went as directed, to Andrew Fornbach. When at once a storm came. On we travelled till we came about a league from Michael Forstern's Inn.

Mar. Who is he?

Bard. A true and faithful brother! There was such a storm, that it was impossible for us to go to Andrew Fornbach's Inn. I made up my mind to go to Michael until the storm stopped. And as we turned in his direction, two soldiers came up so suddenly, that it made Eleanor so frightened, she tried to escape, when her cap flew off and her hair could be seen. The soldiers were astonished at seeing this; and they recognized her as being the daughter of Jacob Olsheim.

Mar. What did they say?

Bard. They said that she is the person they were looking for And they demanded her from me. I told them that she is under my protection, and in a calm way, I said: they can't have her! They said if I do not give her up, they will take me too. I fought like a gentleman, and killed both of them.

Mar. What then did you do.

Bard. I hid their bodies in the woods, and then we went to Michael Forstern. As I was sitting in his inn, all at once three men came in; one was an officer of the inquisition and the other two were soldiers. I was afraid of being found out who we were. I first went to Michael and informed him of my secret, and he said that he would try to do all that was in his power to save the Jewess. Eleanor and Irene put on new disguises and passed off as members of Michael's family. As we were all at supper, the officer of the inquisition asked me where I came from and whither I was traveling. I told him I came from Mannheim, and that I was going to Ulm. But the villian suspected me, for I heard him say that he had seen me not long since in Heidelberg. After supper, as I was going to bed, I heard him say to his companions that the daughter of Jacob Olsheim was beneath Michael's roof. I told Michael they suspected us. He said that he would get some faithful Brothers and arrest the rascals. He went off and I went to sleep—all at once I awoke and found myself a prisoner in the hands of these three men; then they went into the girls' room and also took them prisoners. O, I tell you, my master, I would have given all I had in the world for the use of my right arm and my sword! As the villians were about to take us back to Heidelberg, in marches Michael and some of our brothers. The rascals tried to escape but they could not. Michael and his men fought with them and we killed all three. Then we went to Andrew Fornbach. On my way there we met a poor pilgrim. I have left the girls all safe and here am I.

Mar. By Heavens! there may be something serious grow out of this!

Bard. Still, even if they find that their emissaries have been slain, they cannot trace the deed.

Vic. Unless they bring it home to Michael Forstein.

Bard. I see not how they can do that. To all appearance he is a quiet old man, and surely no one not in the secret would suspect him of such work.

Mar. [*he feels uneasy.*] I don't like to think of that pilgrim. I wish you had found out who and what he was. He may have been a spy.

Vic. We will not worry unnecessarily, and if we think there is danger to the girls where they are, we will move them farther away.

Mar. I will go myself.

Vic. We will decide upon that point some other time. I have an interest in that direction as well as you, for I love my gentle niece.

Mar. We will not beat about the bush. I know you love your gentle niece, and so do I love her—I love her because she is good and true, and generous, and because she has sacrificed so much to serve us. But I love the Jewish maiden with a different love. I love her as man loves but once in a lifetime. If deadly harm should come to her, I should know joy no more on earth.

Vic. I understand you. And you may rest assured that the lovely maiden shall not be deserted. I do not wonder that you love the beautiful Jewess; but, before full success can crown that love, the power of the terrible inquisition must be broken. If you love the maiden with an honorable love——

Mar. Stop! I am not a demon like Berthold of Baden. With my own hands would I sooner pile the green sod upon Eleanor's grave than touch her even with a blightful thought.

Vic. I believe you, my brother. It is not impossible that you may go to Eppingen; but you must not hope too strongly. We have many interests at stake, and in saving one we must not forget the others.

Mar. Forgive me if I have seemed to think too much of myself. Before God I promise you that I have no thought of forsaking our cause, or of allowing anything to draw me from my duty.

Vic. I know it—I know it. But I am sorry that Hector did not make his appearance last night, for I am desirous of hearing from the inquisition. [*a knock*, D. F., *Burdolf opens the door.*]
Enter HECTOR, D. C. F.

Ah, my good lieutenant, you disappointed us last night.

Hec. Business kept me away, and upon that business I have sought you. I discovered early last evening, that something of importance was transpiring, and I was not willing to remain in ignorance. Spies had returned from the east and the Margrave had been sent for. Hour after hour I waited, and at length I gained the knowledge I sought; but when I had gained this it was too late to think of attending our meeting.

Vic. And what was the secret?

Hec. Conrad, through his spies, has made two grand discoveries. First, it had been discovered that four of the Margrave's troopers and one of the messengers of the holy office had been killed in the Black Forest; and second, the hiding place of the Jewess had been discovered.

Mar. [*he starts and is alarmed.*] Do you speak of Eleanor Olsheim?

Hec. Yes.

Mar. Do they know where she is?

Hec. Yes.

Mar. And they have sent their hounds to arrest her?

Hec. They have.

Mar. [*to Victor.*] By the Holy One? I must fly to her assistance; do not say me nay!

Vic. Listen to our lieutenant. He has authority.

Mar. Good Hector, if you have mercy, you will let me go.

Hec. There is danger, Wilsdorf,

Mar. Danger to whom?

Hec. To yourself.

Mar. Out upon trifling, let me go if you love me! I can be discreet. In Heaven's name send me on the mission!

Vic. Let it be as Sir Martin desires; I will not answer for his personal safety, but I will answer for his silence if he is arrested. Let him go, and let Bardolf go with him. [*Victor and Hector both go to door* F.]

Hec. Be it so then. But Sir Martin, be not too hasty. Take your time and you may succeed in saving the Jewess.

Vic. And as soon as you have saved her, let me know. [*Victor and Hector exeunt,* D. F.]

Mar. Bardolf, make yourself ready, and we shall go immediately.

Bard. All right, my master. I am ready. [*both go to the door* F, *in a hurry.*

Mar. In such a cause as this, I feel that I could face the whole force of the inquisition! [*both exeunt,* D. F.]

SCENE V.—*A Street in Heidelberg.*

Enter MARTIN WILSDORF *and* BARDOLF EBERSWALD, L.
[*they look back as they enter.*]

Bard. Easy, my master, we must not attract too much attention.

Mur. We are far enough away. By the mass! I have no heart for lagging now. They who can overtake us must go fast indeed. Come, spare not your feet! [*both rush out* R.]

Enter THERWALD *and five soldiers.* L.

Ther. As I live, there he runs! and with him goes Sir Martin Wilsdorf—our master's brave tutor. By Heavens! I did not expect him to to be at such work. Come my men, and we'll arrest him. [*all exeunt,* R.]

Scene VI.—*Michael Forstern's Inn—Chairs are seen lying about, &c.*

Enter Martin Wilsdorf *and* Bardolf, d. f.

Mar. No one here! [*both look around the stage and open the doors* R. *and* L.] There must have been some alarm. Old Forstern would not thus have deserted his home without unusual cause. Heaven grant that no evil hath befallen him!

Bard. Very likely he has gone to the mountains with his brothers. He must have discovered that this place might not be safe for him.

Mar. We shall gain nothing here, so let us hasten on. My soul! if the other house should be likewise empty!—

Bard. Then we will search farther. [*Bardolf goes to the door* F, *and looks out.*]

Mar. What now?

Bard. We are surrounded!

Mar. Surrounded! By whom?

Bard. By the Margrave's troopers! [*Martin also goes to the door* F.—*he is surprised and both fall back to* L. C.]

Mar. Beim Himmel! We have been tracked hither!

Bard. Yes. They have had their eyes upon this route from the first. They have seen us when we did not see them. Will you surrender?

Mar. Never! To surrender is to die! We had better die here! [*both draw their swords.*]

Therwald *and the five soldiers rush in.*

Ther. Ho, ho! is it you, Wilsdorf?

Mar. You can see for yourself.

Ther. By the mass! I did not think to find my master's brave tutor engaged in such business. But I must perform my duty. You are my prisoner!

Mar. I am the prisoner of no man, unless of my own free will and accord. If you want me you must take me.

Ther. How! Will you resist us?

Mar. You will not take me while I have life!

Ther. By Saint Peter, my good Wilsdorf, you are wild and crazy! You might as well think of escaping the doom of the final day, as to think of escaping the power that now seeks you. Your complicity in this abduction of the Jew's daughter is well known, and there is not a spot in Christendom where your head can be hidden from the Familiars of the Holy Office. I have never borne you any love, nor have I borne you any particular hatred; only I think you have heretofore held your head a little too high; and I am free to confess that it will not pain me to see you slightly humbled. Will you surrender, or must we use force?

Mar. As you please.—But, Therwald, if you advance upon me, you die! [*they both fight—one soldier tries to get behind Martin—Bardolf sees the movement and pushes the soldier back and fights with him and kills him, who falls and dies—Bardolf fights with the others—Martin kills Therwald, who also falls and dies—Martin fights with another, who also falls—as Martin and Bardolf are obout killing two soldiers, in rushes six more soldiers,* D. F.*—they seize Martin and Bardolf—two soldiers are about to dispatch them when* CONRAD *of Marburg rushes in* D. F. *with his sword drawn, and pushes the two soldiers away who were about killing Martin and Bardolf.*]

Con. Back! Back! These men are mine, and he who dares to strike another blow shall suffer with them! Their living tongues are of more use to us than would be a thousand dead men, though in life they had been Christ's most bitter enemies.

[*Picture—Scene closed in.*]

SCENE VII.—*The Woods.*

Enter CONRAD *of Marburg, eight soldiers and* MARTIN *and* BARDOLF, R. *guarded.—All go across the stage and exeuent,* L.

Scene VIII.—*A Chamber in the Castle—a table and two chairs,* R. *a door,* L.—Eleanor *and* Irene *are discovered sitting mournfully.*

Enter a Chambermaid, L. D.

Cham. Can I do anything for your comfort, ladies?

Irene. I know of but one thing. If you will open to us a way of escape from this place, we will bless you.

Cham. Ah, my dears, you don't mean that. Mercy! only think of it! If you were to go away from here you would be taken by the dreadful familiars. Berthold means to be very kind to you—I know he does,—and you ought to be very kind to him. If there's nothing I can do for you, I'll leave you to yourselves, for I know you must be tired.

Irene. You may answer me one question. Where is the Margrave?

Cham. He is not in the castle, but he will be here very shortly; and as he will very likely wish to see you, you had better be prepared for his reception. [*exit* L. D. *and bolts it without.*]

Irene. Don't give up yet. There must be help for us somewhere. Our friends will discover that we have been brought hither.

El. Alas! And what can they do against the power which now holds us! O, Irene, the end is near at hand!

Irene. And let us pray that it may be a peaceful end. Come come, we have one true friend left. We may look to God when all other hope fails us.

El. Dear Irene, you and I are not to remain together. I think they will take you away from me, [*a pause,*] You do not answer me, sister. O tell me—do you think they will take you away from me?

Irene. Yes, Eleanor, I fear they will.

El. [*turning pale.*] And when you are gone I wish to die! O, would that I had been permitted to fall asleep with my father!

Irene. Do not talk in that way, there must be help for you somewhere. Our friends will know that you are here, and I believe they will not rest until you are free. And I too, have need of the same hope. Let us not despair.

El. Yes, yes, dear Irene; you are in danger, but not in such danger as that which threatens me. O, my soul! I cannot bear the thought!

Irene. Sweet sister, I know to what you allude. If I am taken away from you, you must be firm. Hold out to the end if you can, and let that end be——

El. [*draws a dagger from her bosom.*] See! In the last extremity, this shall be my friend!

Irene. You are right; but you will rest 'till the last moment. O, all is not yet lost. The wicked fiends shall not triumph—hark! some one comes.

El. 'Tis the Margrave! [*she replaces the dagger in her bosom.*] *Enter the* CHAMBERMAID, *followed in by* BERTHOLD, L. D.

Ber. [*to Irene.*] So, so, you are the daughter of our bold and trusty servant, Sir Victor.

Irene. No sir,—I am his niece.

Ber. Ah, I remember. But it is all the same. I will converse with you by and by; but for the present my business is with this other lady. You may leave us; this woman will show you which way to go. [*a pause.*] Girl! shall I call in my servants? They are at hand.

El. [*aside to Irene.*] Go; I will be firm. [*Irene exit slowly* L. D. *followed off by the Chambermaid. Berthold closes the door after them.*]

Ber. Lady, if you fear me, you fear without just cause. Your fate is in your own hands, and I tell you the truth when I tell you that you may yet be the happiest of women. [*he takes a seat.*] I have a few questions to ask, and much of your future good may depend upon the answers you give. In the first place I wish to ask concerning property which your father left behind him. You are probably aware that all his earthly possessions belong to the church, It is well known that he possessed much wealth, and it is also known that his wealth was largely invested in jewels of the most valuable kind. Search has been made, but those jewels cannot be found. Can you tell us where they are?

El. I can tell you nothing.

Ber. Ah, my good lady, you do not stop to consider. I fear you do not understand me. You evidently regard me as one of those who were instrumental in your father's misfortune, but you are sadly mistaken. I am your friend, and if you answer me truly I can save you from the most terrible trial. Through my intercession you were brought hither instead of being conveyed to the inquisition: but if I fail in my kind endeavors to gain from you the knowledge I seek, then the inquisitor will claim you at my hands; By Saint Peter, my sweet lady, if you have the least idea of what the inquisition is, you will not throw yourself into its terrible jaws! If you do not answer me, you will be forced to answer the inquisitor. Do you imagine that you could hold your tongue in the hands of the executioners? O, ye Gods! Tongue cannot describe the more than mortal torture to which you may be subjected. Mercy! that sweet lady must not be racked and torn and annihilated by the red-handed fiends. Tell me, I pray you, where your father's wealth is. Tell me, so that I may save you!

El. My lord, suppose I knew where my father, if he had much wealth, had hidden it; and suppose I should tell the secret to you —what then would become of me?

Ber. You should be saved.

El. Saved from what?

Ber. From the dreadful doom of the Inquisition.

El. And what then should be my fate?

Ber. By the gods! you should choose your own fate.—You should be the envy of all the maidens in Heidelberg! Come, tell me where your father's wealth is concealed. I do not wan't it—not a ducat—but the holy office must have it; and if I can lead them to it, they will spare you. Sweet lady, consider. You have a rare power in your hands at this moment. [*He starts from his seat and approaches Eleanor.*]

El. Back! back, sir!

Ber. What, lady—do you fear me?

El. I shall not fear you if you do not touch me.

Ber. By the holy saints! You are as perplexing as you are beautiful! But, I am going to make you love me.

El. Touch me not, sir! Give to me the Inquisition if you will. I had rather be there than be in this castle.

Ber. Poor fool! The inquisitiors will question you through all the tortures your body can bear, and then they will return you to me. If you force me to tell you the whole truth, you can have it in a very few words. You are mine—mine as long as I will. The inquisitior will give you up to me when he has done with you; and you can make me hate you if you please. [*He approaches her again.*] By the holy mother, I'll taste those sweet lips of yours in token of my possession!

[*As he approaches, Eleanor draws the dagger from her bosom —Berthold is surprised and stands* c.] In mercy's name, what will you do with that dagger?

El. I will strike you if I can. If I cannot, then I will strike myself.

[*A knock* L. D.

Ber. Who comes there?

Enter THE CHAMBERMAID, L. D.

Cham. My lord, Conrad of Marburg is below, and wishes to see you.

Ber. Tell him I will be with him instantly. [*exit Chambermaid*, L. D. *bowing to Eleanor.*] Put up that dagger, lady, and rest awhile. I shall see you again, and I trust I may then find you in a more reasonable mood. [*exeunt* L. D. *Eleanor sinks on a seat weeping.*]

Scene IX.—*A Plain Chamber.*

Enter Conrad *of Marburg and* Berthold *the Margrave,* R.

Con. No, no! You must not press your claims to this girl so hotly. You shall have her in the end; but we have use for her here first. I tell you, my lord, there is a deep-laid conspiracy—a conspiracy against the church itself,—and we must ferret it out.

Ber. But, what can the Jewess know of this?

Con. She may know much.

Ber. Pshaw! Do you think conspirators, with their eyes open, would trust their secrets in the keeping of a weak girl?

Con. Perhaps not willingly; but I know that these same conspirators have been instrumental in keeping the girl from us. Two of them we have already, and two more are being looked after.—Martin Wilsdorf and Bardolf Eberswald are safely under lock and key; and we shall soon have possession of the bold Knights, Victor and Baldwin.

Ber. Why not question Wilsdorf at once?

Con. I shall question him, but not alone. The Jewess must bear him company.

Ber. The Jewess?—Do you mean my Jewess?

Con. I mean Eleanor Olsheim.

Ber. But, Conrad, what means this?

Con. Can you not guess?

Ber. Indeed I cannot.

Con. Then listen. I wish to ascertain from the Jewess where her father's money is hidden; and I wish to ascertain from Wilsdorf concerning this conspiracy. The girl may die beneath the torture before she will answer me; but will she see Wilsdorf die when a word of hers can save him?

Ber. Eh! How is that?

Con. It is simply this. Though the girl may look coldly upon you, she bears no such feeling towards this young and gallant Knight. Ye gods, look at the blood he has shed in her service! Even our own faithful Walter is among the victims who have fallen beneath his sword.

Ber. Death! Does the girl love this fellow?

Con. Aye, that she does, my lord.

Ber. Then let her be brought to see him tortured. By the mass, Conrad, you have hit the matter truly. The deeper her love for the Knight, the deeper shall be her torture, when she sees him put to the rack. Spare him not, but let him be twisted and crushed till the thing she has loved loses all human shape! So much for the love that would lead her to spurn me!

Enter a FAMILIAR, R.

Fam. Victor of Antioch and Baldwin of Tyre cannot be found.

Con. Not be found!

Fam. Search has been made, my master.

Con. Never mind—they cannot escape. The bold Knight, Sir Martin Wilsdorf, and Bardolf Eberswald will do for to-night.

[*All exeunt* R.

SCENE X.—*Chambers of the Inquisition. Conrad of Marburg and Berthold the Margrave are discovered.*
(*See Scene V.—Act II.*)

Enter ELEANOR *guarded by two familiars—they lead her to* R. *She looks on the floor.*

Con. Eleanor Olsheim! [*Eleanor looks up.*] You are in

the presence of those who can temper justice with mercy; who can give life, or give death. We have some questions to ask, and we hope you will answer us of your own free will, for we have no desire to put you to the torture. First: Do you know where your father concealed his wealth?

El. I can tell you nothing.

Con. Must we submit you to the torture?

El. I am in your power.

Con. You know not the pain, the terrible agonizing torments of this place. Answer me, and you shall go hence in peace. Refuse, and you may die.

El. I can die, sir.

Con. Lady, you surely know nothing of the torture to which you may here be subjected; and in order that you may gain some idea thereof, we will torture a victim in your presence. This victim is to be a stout, strong man, and when you behold the agony to which we will bring him, you may form some conception of what you may escape if you will. And in this connexion I will give you a rare power of clemency. When you behold the poor wretch in his writhing pain, you may save him at any moment.—When from your lips drop the words that shall lead us to your father's hidden treasure we will release the sufferer. Now we shall witness the depth of your humanity. [*He claps once with his hands—bell tolls* 1.]

Enter MARTIN WILSDORF, L. *guarded by two familiars—they lead him to* C. *Eleanor at seeing Martin expresses astonishment—and rushes to his side—the two familiars that held her, also rush and take her away from Martin.*

El. O! Martin! Martin!

Con. Martin Wilsdorf. [*Martin looks around and gazes at Berthold.*] We know there is a deep-laid conspiracy in our midst, and that its object is to break down the power of the church in the empire. Is there not an orginization in this city with such an aim?

Mar. Why do you ask me that question?

Con. No matter. Will you answer me directly?

Mar. I know of no plan such as you have mentioned.

Con. Are you a member of a secret society in Heidelberg?

Mar. You waste time, sir, in such questioning. I shall answer you nothing.

Con. We'll see. Take this man to the rack, my men, and put forth your strength. Let the victim feel what 'tis to dispise our authority. Ply the bars, and tear him limb from limb!

[*bell tolls* 2.

As the familiars seize Martin and drag him off L. E.—*Eleanor pushes the two familiars away and falls on her knees before Conrad.*]

El. Mercy! Mercy?—Spare him! Spare him! I will tell you all!—you shall find my father's wealth!

Mar. [*without*, L.] Eleanor, trust them not! Speak not a word; let me die where I am—we shall meet in a better world than this!

Con. Down with the wretch! [*the familiars again seize Eleanor and hold her—Enter a Familiar,* R. 1 E] How now, villian?

Fam. We are surrounded by a furious mob, my master!

Con. Ha! Has the foul egg been already hatched? But they cannot gain entrance here.

Fam. They have gained entrance to the inner court, and they are led by some one who has keys to all the doors!

Con. Then, by Heaven, we have had traitors in our very midst! [*Conrad and Berthold rush from their seats and draw their swords.*] My men, strike any man!

Scene X.] THE JEWESS OF HEIDELBERG. 105

[*Enter in a hurry* R. 1 E. ANDREW FORNBACH—MICHAEL FORSTERN—*Brothers of the Steel Cross, headed by* SIR JOSEPH NERDIN, VICTOR *of Antioch,* BALDWIN *of Tyre and* HECTOR *holding the banner which represents the Steel Cross and Sword—all are armed with swords—the Brothers of the Steel Cross fight with the Soldiers and Familiars—Sir Joseph Verdin fights with Berthold and kills him—Hector fights with Conrad and kills him—Eleanor at seeing Victor of Antioch, rushes to his side—she converses with him and both exeunt* L. E.—*all the Familiars and Soldiers fall and dies—re-enter Victor and Eleanor with Martin—enter Bardolf and Irene,* L.—*they shake hands with all—Martin also shakes hands with all—Hector stands waving the banner over the body of Conrad.*

Hec. Thank God that mine has been the hand to free Germany from the presence of this monster!

Mar. Eleanor! Eleanor! Look up sweet love! O, you are saved—saved to bless me forever more! But my love have you got that Cross which I gave you some time ago? [*Eleanor takes from her neck the Cross and shows it to him.*] Now my cup of joy runneth over!

El. Henceforth and forevermore, we are one in Faith as in Love.

TABLEAUX.

DISPOSITION OF THE CHARACTERS.

BROTHERS OF THE STEEL CROSS.

ANDREW.		MICHAEL.
VICTOR.	BARDOLF.	VERDIN.
ELEANOR AND MARTIN.		BALDWIN AND IRENE.
SOLDIERS.	HECTOR.	SOLDIERS.
FAMILIARS.	CONRAD OF MARBURG.	BERTHOLD.
R.	C.	L.

THE END.

www.ingramcontent.com/pod-product-compliance
Lightning Source LLC
Chambersburg PA
CBHW030409170426
43202CB00010B/1544